SOMEWHERE TO BE

BRIAN MOSES

These teaching materials have been produced with the generous support of Reed International.

REED INTERNATIONAL

© WWF UK (World Wide Fund For Nature) 1992

All rights reserved. No part of this publication may be reproduced, stored in a retrieval system, or transmitted in any form or by any means electronic, mechanical, photocopying, recording or otherwise, without the prior permission of WWF UK.

WWF UK
Panda House
Weyside Park
Godalming
Surrey
GU7 1XR

ISBN: 0 947613 61 7

Designed by Schermuly Design Co., London
Cover illustration by Jane Ray
Printed by Hillman Printers, Frome

CONTENTS

A Green Prayer **6**

Introduction **8**

A Threatened World? **10**

Development **30**

Transport **45**

Atmospheric Pollution **57**

Energy Demands **68**

The Food Debate **78**

Animal Rights **94**

The Web of Life **118**

Appendix: A Class Museum or Display **138**

Further Reading Resources for Children and Teachers **139**

Further Addresses for Resource Materials **140**

Acknowledgements **143**

Postscript **144**

A Green Prayer

Save me a clean stream, flowing
to unpolluted seas;

lend me the bare earth, growing
untamed flowers and trees.

May I share safe skies
when I wake, every day,

with birds and butterflies?
Grant me a space where I can play

with water, rocks, trees and sand;
lend me forests, rivers, hills and sea.

Keep me a place in this old land
somewhere to grow, somewhere to be.

Jane Whittle

Attainment targets which children may be helped to acheive at Key Stage 2 through work suggested in *Somewhere To Be*.

AT1 - Speaking and Listening

	a	b	c	d	e	f
Level 2	▓	▓	▓	▓	▓	
3	▓	▓	▓	▓		
4	▓	▓	▓	▓		
5	▓	▓	▓	▓		

AT2 - Reading

	a	b	c	d	e	f
Level 2				▓	▓	▓
3	▓	▓	▓	▓	▓	▓
4	▓	▓	▓	▓		
5	▓	▓	▓	▓	▓	

AT3 - Writing

	a	b	c	d	e	f
Level 2	▓	▓	▓	▓		
3	▓	▓	▓	▓	▓	
4	▓	▓	▓	▓	▓	
5	▓	▓	▓	▓	▓	

INTRODUCTION

**So if we sell you our land, love it as we've loved it.
Care for it as we've cared for it.
Hold in your mind the memory of the land as it is when you take it.
And with all your strength, with all your mind, with all
your heart, preserve it for your children...**

The above words are taken from Chief Seattle's message to the government in Washington DC when they requested to purchase the lands of his people in the mid 1850s.

Native Americans considered the land to be sacred. The mountains, the people, the birds, the air, the rivers – all were interdependent; all were part of the same family. The people of the Chipko movement in India recognised the link between their own well-being and that of their environment when they hugged the trees to prevent their forests from being cut down. It has taken more than a century for such notions to be understood, as until recently, a fragmented view of the world ensured that different interest groups were able to exploit different areas of the natural environment without any thought for the effects that their actions might have on others. However, the past two decades have witnessed widespread recognition of the fact that our actions and lifestyles have caused environmental problems so immense as to threaten the very future of our planet. It is only now, through such realisation, that there is any hope for solutions to the problems we face; problems which are both complex and controversial.

Jonathan Porritt writes that the ecological crisis we are now facing is, in reality, "... a crisis of the human spirit, a crisis which coincides with a period when so many people are already seized by a sense of purposelessness and profound alienation... it is in learning to heal the wounds we have inflicted on the Earth that we may eventually learn to heal our own self-inflicted wounds".[1]

Through the process of education we must ensure that children can begin to tackle the problems they will inherit. There must be an examination of the ways in which we interact with the environment and the motives that lead us to behave in certain ways. There must also be a programme for developing skills and viewpoints that will assist children in assessing their own

---

[1] From Jonathan Porritt's introduction to *The Books for Keeps Green Guide to Children's Books* (BFK, 1991).

relationships with the environment, both locally and globally. This will help them to identify their level of commitment to the environment and to decide how they might wish to modify their own behaviour.

There are no easy answers about many environmental issues and children should understand that people may argue from different, but equally legitimate points of view. Where possible, there should be considerable emphasis on investigation and enquiry through first-hand experience, leading to the development of a personal response to the environment through debate or written work. Much of the poetry and prose included in *Somewhere To Be* may well act as stimuli to writing in the classroom.

Children's responses to the problems that beset our planet are informed and influenced by television, and their beliefs about green issues can have a great effect on their parents. Market researchers are convinced that children play a key role in the green shopping revolution, often demanding that their parents buy environmentally friendly products. Children are also certain as to the kind of future they want for themselves and their children: "... a world where people work in harmony, loving and always equal... a world that's unpolluted, beautiful and free, safe from rubbish and waste, free from hazards..." (Martina Hardiman), "...clean with no litter, rainforests galore, no one who is sick or poor, nothing extinct...." (Claire Hoggins).

The lines written by Martina and Claire echo those written in the mid 1850s by Chief Seattle:

> **And what is there to life if a man cannot hear**
> **the lonely cry of a whippoorwill or the arguments**
> **of the frogs around a pond at night?**

Through a commitment to environmental education we may yet make it possible for the frogs to make themselves heard.

Brian Moses

A Threatened World?

On the twelfth day of Christmas
a human sent to me, 12 pythons,
11 dead snow leopards, 10 canisters
of lead petrol, 9 dying elephants,
8 starving refugees, 7 forests blazing,
6 neutron bombs, 5 crashing Boeing 747s,
4 junk yards, 3 bursting oil pipes,
2 nuclear bombs and a partridge in a
cage underneath a pear tree.

Ben O'Malley

I asked children in Year 6 at Little Ridge School in St Leonards-on-Sea to identify their main areas of environmental concern. Their lists included starvation, things that aren't ozone-friendly, rainforest destruction, litter, pollution, wars, cruelty to animals, nuclear power and so on. A class vote then decided which areas would be the biggest problems that would need to be tackled over the next generation:

1. Starvation
2. Pollution
3. The Ozone Layer
4. Acid Rain
5. Nuclear Power.

We then considered how these problems might be dealt with, although there was a general feeling that children had little say and that their views wouldn't be treated as important. Many environmental issues appear so vast that they often seem totally beyond the power of individuals to make any impact whatsoever. So are we all powerless in the face of immense threats to the existence of life on our planet, or can we all do something at local level which may just have a knock-on effect?

Read the poem below and ask children whether they think that the attitude expressed is one that is shared by many people today. What factors prevent people from getting involved? Could these be listed in some sort of order?

Names

My name is 'Couldn't care less',
just let the forests die.
My name is 'Can't be bothered',
who cares about holes in the sky?

My name is 'I'm too busy',
let someone else do the worrying,
there's nothing that I can do
if the ice caps are wearing thin.

My name is 'Leave me alone',
just don't go preaching to me.
Gossip is what I care about
not oil that's spilt in the sea.

My name is 'I'm alright Jack',
there's really no cause for alarm.
Hens are silly birds, who cares
if they suffer at the factory farm?

Who cares about global warming,
I like a spot of hot weather.
My name is 'Sit on the fence',
my name is 'All of a dither'.

So stop saying what I should think,
I don't want to believe what I'm told.
My name is 'Hope it will go away',
My name is 'Don't get involved'.

And who do you think you are,
telling us all we should worry?
*WELL MY NAME'S A WARNING FROM FUTURE YEARS,
IT'S 'LISTEN OR YOU'LL BE SORRY'.*

Brian Moses

Perhaps a reply might be written to the above, using the same structure but thinking of positive names:

My name is 'Always recycle'
I collect up bottles and cans.
My name is 'Friend to the Earth',
I'm one of its biggest fans!

David Hicks, Project Director of the Global Futures Project, writes: "There is always a danger when we teach about global issues that we make children feel disempowered rather than empowered. This is why it is crucial to read case studies of success stories: examples of children and adults, individuals, groups and governments working to create a better world. Often such stories are small scale, but that is where we have to begin."

Ordinary people can make a difference. If we educate ourselves to what is happening in the world, then our arguments can be more persuasive, giving us more power to get things changed. Ask children to discuss and then list the various ways in which we receive information about environmental issues. Set up a notice board where newspaper articles can be displayed. Half the board could be for pessimistic items and the other half for success stories. Which side fills up first? Make a list of the questions that children would like to ask about their world. Sub-divide these into subject areas – the food we eat, the products we buy, the transport we use, the resources we have left, species under threat. How many questions lead to answers that can't be resolved? Are there measures that individuals can take – writing to firms, writing to politicians, choosing to boycott products? Individual example encourages others and awareness spreads from families to friends, then to their families and so on.

A report from market researchers Mintel (Autumn 1991) claims that children's beliefs about green issues are spreading to their parents. Many have been persuaded into buying environmentally-friendly products through pressure from their children. Many firms have recognised that more and more people are demanding such products and are starting to meet that demand.

Writing about various issues can help children to clarify their feelings and to develop an appreciation that our environment is important:

Why Our Planet?

Why do we ruin our Earth so quick
With chain saws and oil slicks,

Carbon-dioxide and CFC'S,
Killing animals, cutting down trees,

Spraying pesticides on crops and land,
Soon our world will be just desert and sand.

You call technology a success,
We've made our world a terrible mess.

But look carefully at the progress we've made.
We all need to work together for the world to be saved.

Gemma Finney, 10 years

Thoughtless Humans

They don't care for birds and mammals,
No they don't care a bit for wildlife.
They only give homes to people with money,
Yes all they think of is war and strife.

They don't care for trees and plants,
No they don't care a bit for growing things.
They cut down trees for homes for humans,
And never seem to think of the sadness it brings.

They don't care for frogs and toads,
No they don't care a bit for the water habitat.
They pollute the water with all their rubbish,
So what do you think about that?

Laura Shuff, 10 years

Captain Eco and the Fate of the Earth, written by Jonathan Porritt and illustrated by Ellis Nadler (Dorling Kindersley, 1991), tells of the adventures of Captain Eco as he sets off on a mission to save the Earth. With him are two Earthlings, Michelle and Clive. Captain Eco shows the Earthlings just what will happen to their planet if they fail to take heed of his dire warnings. The comic book format of the book makes it an attractive read for even reluctant readers and the various messages are put across most effectively. Many children will want to take Captain Eco on further adventures or to devise their own comic book heroes and protectors of the environment:

Man is trying to destroy our world. Then two creations come out of the sea. One is Eddie the Environment and the other is Ollie the Oil Slick.

One day Ollie the Oil Slick decided to create some acid rain. Just outside was Eddie the Environment. He started to bash against Ollie's door. Soon he smashed it down. He burst in and shouted, 'Hold it right there!'. 'No' shouted Ollie. So Eddie the Environment pushed Ollie the Oil Slick into the acid rain.

Christopher Kinlan, 9 years

Humour might also be used in other writing tasks where children are encouraged to explore various issues and to promote a message in an imaginative way. In the piece below, Imogen is advertising for a caretaker to look after the Earth:

WANTED - A CARETAKER

The requirements for this job aren't really for some bloke who enjoys plodding about in an ovaltine coloured overcoat.

What is needed is a **Superhuman**.

For this position you will need to have studied: History, Geography, Languages, Science and Persuasion.

You will also need to be able to fly an aeroplane, drive a lorry full of elephants without having a nervous breakdown, navigate a speedboat fast enough to block the way of a 5,000 ton oil tanker with a leak in it and dive while disguising yourself as a porpoise.

You will also have to have the strength to block up the chimneys of a power station. You will need to be able to get to Asia and Australia in one week. You will have access to the cleaning cupboard at all times. Also you will have to be able to handle Rotweillers well enough to be the international distributor of supersonic portable recycling plants (the kind that fit onto the sides of hostess trolleys).

Applications **must** be in by the beginning of an outbreak of pollution.

Imogen Hibbert, 11 years

In the following piece, Aaron writes the kind of letter that the Earth might compose if it were writing to an agony aunt and complaining about all the problems that beset it:

Dear **Great Green Argulschnezer,**
I am a small green-blue planet in the unfashionable end of the western spiral arm of our galaxy. I am very unfortunate as the ape descendants who live on me keep pumping CFCs, fumes and smoke into my atmosphere. I've even got a bald spot over one of my icy countries. Also they're cutting down masses of my forests, soon I'll have to buy a continental wig. Then they dig up my oil and metal. Different countries have wars and

they fire missiles at each other that are so accurate they can hit a garage door 600 kilometres away, then they drop bombs. They also drop rubbish in my seas and oceans.

Please help me.

Blue-Green Planet.

Aaron Turpin, 12 years

It is doubtful whether the Great Green Argulschnezer's reply was of much comfort to the Earth. It merely reminded our planet that it is much better off than those which have been disintegrated to make way for a hyperspace by-pass!

After reading and looking at Captain Eco's exploits, and perhaps attempting something similar to one of the above examples themselves, children could discuss whether there is a place for humour when writing about serious ecological concerns and if so, whether it can be used to put over a message.

Another way to encourage exploration of environmental concerns is to take up a standpoint from some time in the future. The poet Kevin McCann writes about the items that might be exhibited in a Museum of Past Centuries:

In the Museum of Past Centuries

We have
Elephant tusks, a grey seal,
The songs of the Blue Whale,
White snow, green fields,
The Rain Forest's very last tree.

In the Museum
of Past Centuries

We have
English wolves,
Dodo birds,
Aztecs, Incas,
Tasmanian Aborigines

> In the Museum
> of Past Centuries
>
> We have
> Stinking rivers,
> Acid lakes,
> Dying fish,
> Dead seas.
>
> In the Museum
> of Past Centuries
> We have
>
> Mustard gas,
> Barbed wire,
> Atom bombs,
> A lead container
> Marked 'Deadly'.
>
> In the Museum
> of Past Centuries
>
> We have
> *(Standing alone)*
> A single glass case,
> Inside, an apple
> That's been bitten twice:
> Old, tempting and juicy.
>
> **Kevin McCann**

Kevin McCann writes of the above poem: "The Museum of Past Centuries contains the things that in this century we're in danger of losing, the things that in Past Centuries we've lost and the things that are helping to destroy our planet. The apple tree stands for choice. As human beings we have a simple choice – we can destroy our planet or we can save it. Which one is it going to be?"

Children could be asked to make lists of what they would find in such a museum. These could then be included in a poem or as part of a story in which future beings discover a building that houses such a museum. Each item would provide clues to the creatures who once lived on our planet.

In the title story of Louise Lawrence's book of science fiction stories, *Extinction is Forever* (Red Fox, 1991), Stephen is transported through time to a drowned London where he learns of man's folly from the amphibious inhabitants. He is determined to return and warn of the bleak future to come but finds instead that he is stranded in the future. The message, of course, is that no one should be allowed to tamper with the past. The story should promote much discussion and written work about where we are heading, and although in this instance the world was destroyed in a nuclear holocaust, it doesn't take much imagination to picture a bleak future resulting from total neglect of our planet's well-being.

Children could be asked to express their feelings of regret in the form of a poem with the repeating line, *If I could turn back time ...*

If I Could Turn Back Time

If I could turn back time
I would take the pollution out of the sea.
I would knock down cars, not trees,
I would take London and vacuum up the mess.
Recycle! Recycle!

If I could turn back time
I would make a new start on life.
Wipe out leaded petrol,
Close up the hole in the ozone layer.
Recycle! Recycle!

If I could turn back time
I'd bring back the dodo,
They got wiped out by us bozos.
Restart a life or extinct species.
Recycle! Recycle!

Ben Jacques, 10 years

Children might also write a letter to their grandchildren, setting out what they would like them to inherit – clean water, clean air, clean soils etc. Alternatively they might compose a letter from their grandchildren set in the future, asking them why nothing was done to curb pollution in its many forms. Organise a role play, set at some stage in the future, in which visitors from space explain to people from Earth about the world that they are from and how it is so much better than what they find happening on Earth. Other children could try and explain that although Earth has been neglected and abused, there are still some things that are worth preserving.

The poems by Kevin McCann and Brian Jacques, although rather gloomy in outlook, do at least have the desired effect of making us think about where we are heading. This is also true of the following poem:

Nostalgia

'The other man's grass is always greener.'
That takes me back.

We used to say
'The other man's grass is always greener'

or we would say
'The grass is always greener on the other side'
when we were feeling envious or dissatisfied.

We meant that,
even if our plates were piled up
with glorious food,
the person at the next table
always seemed to be eating something tastier
or however fast our car would go,
our neighbour's car would go faster.

That was the trouble –
we never were satisfied.
We always wanted more.
We always wanted to go faster.

Anyway, off you go.
I can see that you're bored.

Tell you what though,
before you come
to visit me again
I'll find my photo album:
show you some pictures of me
when I was your age.

Pictures of me standing, not on concrete,
but on grass.

I'll expect you'll find it hard to believe
that there was such stuff

and how green it was.

Bernard Young

I many ways Bernard Young's poem echoes the lines from Joni Mitchell's song 'Big Yellow Taxi', "They took all the trees/And put them in a tree museum". Children might be interested to hear this song and to consider what a tree museum might look like. All kinds of writing might follow from this – an account of an expedition to discover the last tree in the world; a letter to the paper from an elderly person who can still remember a world with trees; an encyclopedia entry for trees saying what happened to them, where they may be seen, and what they look like (include a tree identification chart).

Jennifer Tweedie writes about the gradual disappearance of trees in her neighbourhood:

A Story of Trees

There used to be lots of trees near where I live – oaks and beeches and ash and plane. They were lived in by birds and insects and played amongst by children. Nobody wanted them to be destroyed.

When builders bought the land where the trees grew, they promised to keep the trees. They said they would build their homes around them. And they did. Mostly. You never saw the builders cut down a tree, but when the houses were finished, there seemed to be less trees than there had been before.

When the people moved into the houses, they had enormous oak trees in their garden – right up close to their front doors or brushing against their bedroom windows. Most of them liked living amongst trees at first. They hung rope swings on the branches and built tree houses for their children.

But trees block out sunlight. Their roots damage foundations.

Soon the pruning began. After the pruning, the trees didn't seem quite so big, but it didn't keep the people happy for long.

Next came the amputations. Great branches were lopped off. No homes were left for birds and insects, though some of the rope swings remained.

After that the destruction was easy. The trees didn't seem to matter much without limbs. What was the point of a trunk with no branches?

The people weren't supposed to cut down the trees. They had promised not to – sort of. But the Council don't have time to worry about an old oak tree here and there … and there … and there … and there … and there.

Have you got any trees in your neighbourhood? I haven't any left in mine.

Jennifer Tweedie

Are there lots of things changing that we don't really know about until it's too late? Can children think of instances similar to the one related above or is this now too cynical an outlook at a time when people at all sorts of levels have to be much more accountable for their actions, even big business? It isn't difficult, however, to find examples of flagrant disregard for the environment – oil being dumped at sea or chemicals discharged into rivers and streams. Have children seen examples of polluted water? Such instances should be reported to the National Rivers Authority or the local Environmental Health Officer.

Read and discuss the following poem which relates to an incident of stream pollution:

Blood Stream

We used to dam the stream
by Clarke's farm –
till it ran thick with scum
that caught on the reeds
and frothed like bubble bath.

We used to laugh and splash
in the stream by Clarke's farm –
till dark fronds of grey weed
snagged our legs with slime.

We used to paddle in the stream
by Clarke's farm –
till bloated dead fish floated
upside down,
slippery as soap.

We used to play
in Clarke's stream
till something we never saw
swam through the blood stream
and poisoned its rich vein.

Pie Corbett

The above poem might well be used as a springboard for children's own writing, perhaps beginning each verse in a similar way, *We used to play on the beach until... we used to walk in the fields until...*

In the poem below, Shirah and Sarah write their poem in the form of a letter to Mother Nature, from a polluted river:

Dear Mother Nature

Dear Mother Nature,
I'm the polluted river.
I talk to you
because you're the giver.

Rivers can't drown
but this one is.
Under coke cans, nappies,
the usual biz.

How can I survive, tell me how?
I used to be beautiful,
but sadly not now.
Radiation wavers
between my dingy banks.
Steel and plastic kettles,
Russian oil tanks.

Dear Mother Nature,
I'm not the only one.
If the others are feeling like me,
they're not having fun.
The world is dying,
it's truly wrong,
and this is to you mother,
A river's dying song.

Shirah Reel and Sarah Cummings, 12 years

It is well worth trying to obtain a copy of *Mr Noah and the Second Flood* by Sheila Burnford. (The book was first published by Gollancz in 1973, and subsequently by Puffin. Copies may still be found in libraries.) This is a fable concerning the true descendants of the original Noah who still live on the mountain where the Ark came to rest. They farm the land in the traditional way and know very little of what is happening in the outside world. However one day Mr Noah reads about the gradual warming up of the Earth and the increased precipitation that this will bring and becomes convinced that there will be a second flood. He thus sets out to build another Ark and send his sons to spread the news to all the world's creatures.

When the animals gather it is obvious that many of the creatures that travelled with Mr Noah's famous ancestor are missing, particularly the great cats. Finally an old and somewhat shabby tiger limps into view and explains how over-hunting has wiped out various species. When the floodwaters rise they are covered with oil and filled with rubbish. When Mr Noah asks who should be held responsible for the mess, the rather embarrassed tiger mumbles that it all seems to have been achieved by tools. It then dawns on Mr Noah that the original Noah made a big mistake in ensuring the continuance of the human race on Earth. He orders his sons and their wives to leave the Ark and board one of the many rockets that were taking people to new lives on other planets.

Such a tale cannot fail to engender all kinds of discussion about the rights and wrongs of the various issues that are raised, and consideration of these issues may lead children to write down their own observations about places with which they are familiar:

Floating Rubbish Tip

Floating rubbish tip,
Smelly, dirty.
Water looks muddy, oily and murky.
Bits of driftwood,
Rubble and cans.
Bits of a dummy, its body and hand.
Bottles and bubbles
And brown looking foam.
I don't want to see this, I'm going
Home.

John Wells, 10 years

Is 'going home' any sort of an answer or can we all find some small way of helping to stem the rising tide of pollution? Children might care to take part in rubbish clearing exercises. Research shows that 70% of all litter on the beaches of southern England comes from ships and boats. This figure can rise to almost 100% in northern Scotland and although there is an international agreement for the prevention of pollution from ships, there is no effective way of enforcing it. Sometimes there are organised collections of litter where children will be welcome to help, but if such exercises are organised by schools then children should wear gloves and report anything that looks suspicious e.g. syringes found on beaches. Rules and regulations for such activities can be drawn up by the children prior to setting out.

Suggest that children keep "A Diary of a Green Month", in which they record something they do each day, or something they start to do which is helping the environment. Entries may note small measures – taking some cans to the recycling point; or larger endeavours – took part in an organised clearance of rubbish from a stretch of coastline.

Can children produce a list of rules for a 'green thinking person'? What measures should we be taking so that our daily actions are beneficial to the future of our planet? Production of such a list should promote much discussion, particularly if children are limited to ten rules which should neatly encapsulate current thinking on green issues! This list of rules could be written out so that they provide meaningful guidelines for very young children. Suggest that leaflets or posters be prepared that feature the list along will illustrations that might help to make the meaning clearer for anyone with reading difficulties.

Ask children to discuss and then list the various ways in which they can act positively for the benefit of the environment both locally and globally. The list will probably turn out to be quite lengthy. Some of these suggestions could then be acted on in a practical way – setting up recycling points within the school, organising school assemblies which encourage awareness in others, starting up or joining a conservation club, setting up a school nature reserve, writing letters about environmental problems and so on. Keep an eye on the local environment and look for success stories too – rubbish cleared away, an environmentally friendly development, new trees planted etc. Write letters about these too so that others may be encouraged by signs of success or prepare a publicity campaign which focuses on one or more environmental issues.

In the following photographs, Gemma Finney, Alexi Gee and Shaminar Malik from West Hove Junior School designed posters, leaflets and badges as part of their campaigns.

Adresses for Further Information

Ark Trust, 498-500 Harrow Road, London W9 3QA

Community Recycling Opportunities Programme, 7 Burner's Lane, Kiln Farm, Milton Keynes MK11 3HA

Conservation Trust, George Palmer Site, Northumberland Avenue, Reading, Berkshire RG2 7PW

Department of the Environment, 43 Marsham Street, London SW1P 3EB

Friends of the Earth, 26-28 Underwood Street, London WC2N 4HG

Greenpeace, 30-31 Islington Green, London N1 8XE

Men of the Trees, Sandy Lane, Crawley Down, West Sussex, RH10 4HS

Save-a-Can, Elm House, 19 Elmshott Lane, Cippenham, Nr Slough, Berks SL1 5QS

The British Trust for Conservation Volunteers, 36 St Mary's Street, Wallingford, Oxon OX10 0EU

Watch, c/o Royal Society for Nature Conservation, 22 The Green, Nettleham, Lincoln LN2 2NR (young people's conservation group)

Woodland Trust, Autumn Park, Grantham, Lincolnshire NG31 6LL

READING RESOURCES

Poetry

A Fourth Poetry Book compiled by John Foster (OUP, 1982) includes 'The Newcomer' by Brian Patten and 'Fish in a Polluted River' by Ian Serraillier.

Green Poetry selected by Robert Hull (Wayland, 1991) includes 'Big Yellow Taxi' by Joni Mitchell and 'Problems' by Brian Moses.

Spaceways compiled by John Fosters (OUP, 1986) includes 'Do you think we'll ever get to see Earth, sir?' by Sheenagh Pugh.

The Last Rabbit – A Collection of Green Poems, edited by Jennifer Curry (Methuen/Mammoth, 1990) includes 'Space Ark' by Jenny Craig.

What on Earth...? Poems with a Conservation Theme, edited by Judith Nicholls, (Faber, 1989) includes 'Countdown' by Judith Nicholls, 'To Walk on Grass' by Gordon MacIntosh, 'That Last Human' by Louisa-Jane Snook (14 years), and 'Big Yellow Taxi' by Joni Mitchell.

Fiction

Dear Clare, My Ex Best Friend by Ursula Jones (Knight Books, 1991). Thirteen year old Anna Pitts writes letters to her friend Clare in Australia, and also to the Queen and other world leaders asking them what they are going to do about a range of environmental problems.

Once Upon a Planet, short stories about various aspects of the environment selected by Christina Martinez (Puffin, 1989). Includes 'The Glass Cupboard' by Terry Jones, extracts from 'Boy' (Roald Dahl) and 'One-Eyed Cat' (Paula Fox), plus a new story from Jan Mark.

Poll by Avril Rowlands (OUP, 1991). Katie searches for her brother Ben who vanishes along with the local supermarket. She journeys through a strange land of disappearing rainforests and polluted rivers. Along the way Katie realises that she can do something to change things. A thought-provoking read that should promote much discussion.

Save the Human by Tony Husband and David Wood (Antelope Books, Hamish Hamilton, 1992). Animals are in charge of the world and some keep humans as pets. An interesting and entertaining turnaround!

The World that Jack Built written and illustrated by Ruth Brown (Anderson Press, 1990). Based on the rhyme 'The House that Jack Built' this picture book features a black cat exploring two valleys, one unspoilt and the other polluted by a factory built by Jack. Splendid pictures and a powerful message.

Watch Out for the Giant-Killers! by Colin McNaughton (Walker Books, 1991). A small boy meets a green giant in the Amazon forest. The giant tells him how giants were driven from other parts of the world to make new homes in the rainforest, but now even these homes are threatened. Wonderful illustrations and plenty of humour alongside the serious message.

Non-fiction

Environmentally Yours: A Green Handbook for Young People produced by *Early Times* and Puffin (1991). Examines what is happening at the moment and what will happen if things carry on the way they are. Plus 'Towards a Better World' - what we can do to help.

How Green Are You? by David Bellamy (Frances Lincoln, 1991). A well-produced and lively reminder of just how important our efforts are as individuals in any conservation programme. Plenty of practical ideas.

Ian and Fred's Big Green Book by Fred Pearce and Ian Winton (Kingfisher, 1991). An excellent review of the major problems that beset our planet. Inspired by the Gaia hypothesis which maintains that all living things are linked and need to remain in balance to ensure survival. Humans, of course, are altering this fragile balance.

Our Planet – A guide to our world and its changing environment (Picture Pocket, Kingfisher, 1991). Useful survey of environmental problems plus ideas for making changes. Well produced and attractively illustrated.

The Blue Peter Green Book written by three members of the *Blue Peter* team – Lewis Bronze, Nick Heathcote and Peter Brown (BBC Books/Sainsbury's, 1990). An examination of the problems that beset the environment plus 'Action – How you can help' sections.

The Young Green Consumer Guide by John Elkington and Julia Hailes, with Douglas Hill, illustrated by Tony Ross (Gollancz, 1990). A fascinating book that explores the issues and suggests ways in which individuals can help, both practically and through helping to raise awareness.

The Young Person's Guide to Saving the Planet by Debbie Silver and Bernadette Vallely (Virago, 1990). Different forms of action that can be taken plus an A-Z of Green issues from acid rain to zoos, from CFCs to VDUs. Good as a quick reference guide.

50 Simple Things Kids Can Do To Save The Earth written by the Earthworks Group (Sphere Books, 1990). Everything from being a bottle bandit to stamping out styrofoam; from being school-wise to joining the heat-busters, plus eco-experiments – make your own recycled paper etc.

DEVELOPMENT

....

Question children as to what they understand by development. *The Penguin Reference Dictionary* defines 'develop' as "... to build on or change the use of (a tract of land)" and 'development' as "... the act, process or result of developing". Consider whether development should be automatically linked with the concept of progress. Do children feel that development is a good or a bad thing? Can examples of both types of development be found in the local area? What about national or international examples?

"*Developers* have bought the site – don't you know what that means? It means big business, big money. They'll have paid a bomb for it and they'll be planning to make an even bigger bomb when they've built all the houses and flats and sold them. They're not going to be stopped by anything we say."

(From *Awaiting Developments* by Judy Allen, Julia MacRae Books, 1988)

In a class or in groups, try to work out criteria for good development – sensitivity to the environment, providing or maintaining a decent life and livelihood for people, involving local people in planning and design, using appropriate skills and technologies. Consider how large housing estates might be improved – consultation with residents to discuss their requirements, inclusion of social centres where people can meet for different activities, shops, public house, a library, wildlife gardens, community art etc. Such developments can mean huge improvements in the quality of life for the people who live there.

Consider bad or inappropriate development – damaging the environment for short term profits, taking no account of the wishes of local people, importing wholesale systems that are inappropriate to the natural and social environment.

> "What's happening to the village pond then?" The three Garys had just arrived, so I explained what I knew, which wasn't much.
> "Holiday homes?" said Gary One. "Who wants to come here for their holiday? My mum and dad spend all year saving so that we can get away from this dump."
> "Rich people, I suppose," I said. "Looking for a bit of peace and quiet. Getting away from all the traffic in towns."
> "But if they all come here and build houses all over our village, it'll be just as noisy as wherever it is they come from," said Gary Two.
> "Yeah," said Gary Three. "So where's the point in that?"

(From *Mightier than the Sword* by Clare Bevan, Blackie, 1989)

Both of the above extracts are from stories that follow children's crusades against property developers. In *Awaiting Developments*, Jo is attempting to prevent the clearance of a beautiful garden and its subsequent development as a site for houses and flats. She petitions her neighbours in response to a letter from the Council asking if anyone has objections to the plan, but even her father is dismissive of her efforts, telling her that the Council are unlikely to listen anyway, and even less likely to listen to someone who hasn't got a vote.

In *Mightier than the Sword*, Adam suffers with spina bifida and spends most of his time in his wheelchair. However he is very much a gang member and when a property developer threatens to drain the village pond and build houses on the site, Adam's gang join up with 'The Badger Man' to try and prevent it from happening. The story is linked with a re-telling of the Arthurian legends and it is Adam's antique pen *Excalibur* that helps to achieve a victory.

In both of these books, children begin to question how much notice will be taken of their efforts, and Jonathan Porritt's statement, "Umpteen Goliaths have been toppled by community-backed Davids", (*Save the Earth*, Dorling Kindersley, 1991) may prove a useful starting point for class discussion.

Decisions to develop, to build new roads or sites for industry, are often taken by people who live well away from the locality. Thus local people need to make their views known as it is their area that may be changed irreversibly.

Felling Trees

Stop! I cried to them,
>But the noise of their saws
Cut out my final plea.
>Everything is dying:
Dark sky where the flats will be.

Adrian Youd, 12 years (From *What on Earth*, Faber, 1989)

How effective do children feel that any protest would be? Are there local development plans which are threatening the environment in your area? Perhaps the children can identify the advantages and disadvantages of such a scheme. Can the children work out how their locality might be appropriately developed? What could be done to stir up support for a campaign of action? Can petitions be effective? How do children feel about Jo's efforts in *Awaiting Developments*?

Evidence that young people can play an effective part in tackling property developers may be found in an account by *Plus* magazine concerning the activities of 10 year old Marie Palmer who organised a successful campaign to save an area of Berkshire woodland. Marie wrote to the Prime Minister and to Nicholas Ridley, Environment Secretary at the time, both of whom did nothing. She wrote to Prince Charles who was sympathetic. Her efforts came to the attention of her local paper and both television and the National Press took up her cause. The developers and local council were embarrassed by the publicity and were unwilling to press forward with their plans. However, new developers and new plans have since emerged and Marie Palmer is protesting again.

In his novel *The Melanie Pluckrose Effect* (Blackie, 1991), Roger Burt writes about a campaign by four schoolgirls (plus the fictitious Melanie Pluckrose) to save their town centre from the hands of developers. This is both an entertaining and informative read as the story details the various ways in which the girls organise their campaign, keeping it in the public eye through a series of letters to the local newspaper, through the mass production of stickers and T-shirts, and then through the proposal of an alternative plan that takes into account suggestions from residents.

Suggest that children gather information on the ways in which individuals can lodge protests regarding developments with which they disagree. Letters might be written to the Town Hall and Planning Offices asking about correct procedures for submitting protests.

A Department of the Environment booklet – *Local Plans: Public Local Inquiries, A Guide to Procedure*, gives much useful information as to the correct ways to object to development plans. (An address for this booklet appears at the end of this section.) The flow chart below is extracted from the booklet and details the local plan process:

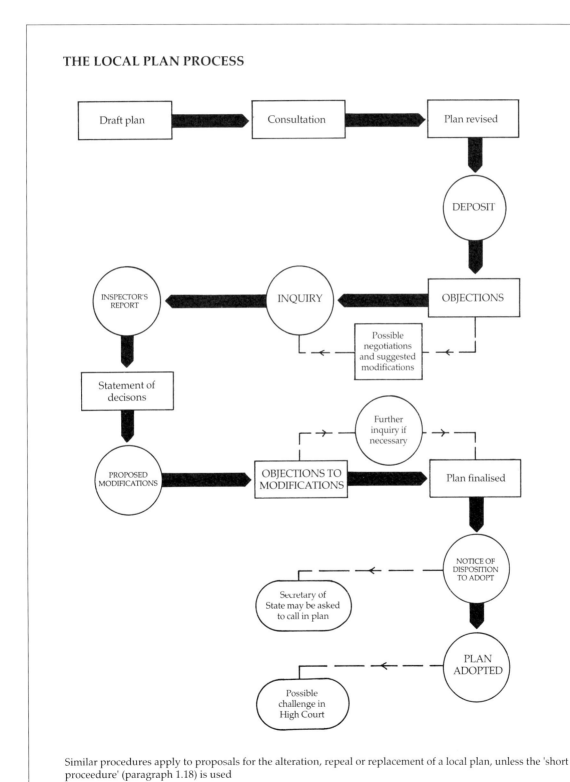

THE LOCAL PLAN PROCESS

Similar procedures apply to proposals for the alteration, repeal or replacement of a local plan, unless the 'short proceedure' (paragraph 1.18) is used

Consider the poem by Raymond Wilson, 'This Letter's to Say' which may be found in *A Fourth Poetry Book* edited by John Foster (OUP), in *What on Earth...?* edited by Judith Nicholls (Faber) and in *Green Poetry* selected by Robert Hull (Wayland).

The poem is written in the form of a letter informing the owner of a house that his or her property is about to be knocked down as it stands in the path of a new motorway. New accommodation is offered three miles away on the thirteenth floor of a tower block. "There is no appeal", the letter says.

Discuss the poem and try to empathise with the way in which the property owner would feel, particularly if the letter's recipient was an old person. Can anything be done to prevent the development? Children may like to take this as a starting point and to mount a campaign to save the property.

ADAM AND PARADISE ISLAND

Written and illustrated by Charles Keeping (OUP, 1989), *Adam and Paradise Island* is a picture book for all ages. It concerns a small island in the middle of a muddy creek, linked to either side by stone bridges. There are lovely illustrations showing the shops and storekeepers who trade on the island, and of two former itinerants – Old Varda and Ma Burley who live there. To the council, Paradise Island is a mess and a decision is taken to build a fast toll road across the island linking both sides of the creek. Adam loves the island and is dismayed to see all the destruction taking place. However, while the road is being built, Adam and his friends, with the help of Old Varda and Ma Burley, are busy salvaging an area of the island and turning it into a children's playground.

Characters:
Adam *(9 or 10 years old)*
Sarah Sprout *(greengrocer)*
Bertie Bull *(butcher)*
Percy Pike *(fishmonger)*
Betty Bun *(cake shop)*
Old Varda *(former traveller, now living on the island with his caravan, pony and cart, goat and chickens)*
Ma Burley *(former traveller on rivers and canals, now living in her houseboat with her dog and two caged birds)*
Council members: Mayor Sir Cecil Bland, Major Blanco, The Honourable Claude Berk, Ernie Blunt, Sybil Sillie, Lady Primrose *(all these vote for the new road)*
Bernie Black, Winnie White *(both vote against the scheme)*
Gerry Bandynose *(TV and radio idol)*

The following ideas and activities can be linked to the story:

1. Character descriptions, past histories, families, jobs etc.
2. Announcement of Council's intentions towards Paradise Island a) in the local paper, and b) on local radio.
3. Letters of protest from shopkeepers complaining of loss of livelihood.
4. Letters from councillors replying to shopkeepers promising them new jobs in the mainland's Neata Supermarket.
5. Tape recorded interviews with Old Varda and Ma Burley to assess their reactions.
6. List of reasons for the project and reasons against.
7. Acting out a Council meeting with Bernie Black and Winnie White objecting.
8. Posters announcing a public meeting to discuss the plans.
9. Placards and banners with slogans e.g. SAVE PARADISE ISLAND etc.
10. Considering the plight of wildlife on the island. Write a reasoned letter of protest.
11. Drama – planning the playground (Adam, his friends plus Old Varda/Ma Burley).
12. Annotated plan of the proposed play area – activities, safety features etc.
13. Poster – Grand Opening of the new toll road by Gerry Bandynose.
14. Newspaper biography of Gerry Bandynose, TV and radio idol.
15. Reports of the opening and of the disgraceful scenes that take place in
    a) the newspaper, and b) local radio.
16. Notice of toll charges for the new road.
17. Neata Supermarket – opening offers, advertisement, radio jingle.

In addition, some of the general activities listed below could be undertaken:

1. Design new book covers.
2. Retell the story.
3. Storyboard – tell the story in eight captioned pictures. What <u>must</u> be included, what will have to be left out?
4. Think of questions that could have been put to the author/illustrator if he had still been alive.
5. Draw your favourite character.
6. Write a character's diary for a day in the story.
7. Tell the story to someone who hasn't heard it.
8. Draw a map to show where the activities took place.
9. Describe what happens from a particular character's viewpoint.
10. Write a sequel.

Reservoirs

When we consider how often it rains in Britain, it seems ridiculous to think that we could ever face a serious water shortage. However, many areas of England have recently experienced three consecutive summers of drought and groundwater reserves are lower than they have ever been before. Some parts of the country rely on groundwater for up to 70% of supplies. The problem is further exacerbated by poor distribution and a lack of adequate storage facilities. It is a mammoth task to collect the water, store it, treat it and then distribute it to homes and industries. Added to this is the fact that demand for water in England and Wales has risen by 70% over the past 30 years.

There are now plans for water companies to build five new reservoirs in the south of England which will swallow up huge areas of countryside. Such proposals inevitably arouse great anger among conservationists and local residents. When plans were announced to flood part of the North Tyne Valley in Northumberland so that the Kielder Dam and reservoir might be constructed, there were public protests from the residents who faced the loss of homes and livelihoods.

Today, however, water companies do pay more attention to environmental considerations and attempt to find sites where whole villages will not have to be submerged or dams built with little regard as to how they fit in with the surrounding countryside. But conservationists still have valid arguments:

"There are 400 year-old oaks, dormice and honey buzzards. I have spent hours watching the muntjac deer and in the spring the woods are a carpet of bluebells. Who in their right mind would want to destroy all this?"

(Mrs Candida Parminter, 90 years old, explaining in *Green Magazine* how South West Water Services are aiming to submerge 22 hectares of the Higher Bruckland valley in southeast Devon, while the water company state that the project is needed so that hosepipe bans do not become an annual event.)

A New Reservoir?

Inform your children that their local water company is proposing to flood a large area of the countryside so that a dam and a reservoir can be built to supply water to nearby towns and cities. What can they infer from the initial proposal? Do they foresee any problems?

Allow the children to consider the views of both sides of the argument. The water company knows that a reservoir is needed to prevent water shortages. It will provide employment in the area and the completed reservoir can be used for leisure activities. However, those people living close by are concerned about the disappearance of a large area of land, its history and ecology, and in some instances perhaps even the loss of a home or livelihood.

After initial discussion on the issue and perhaps a vote, divide the class into two camps. This may happen naturally; but more than likely, so that numbers are fairly even, some children will find themselves arguing from points of view that they didn't support in the vote. This can be a valuable exercise in itself.

Those who oppose the scheme might form a preservation society, list the arguments against the scheme and decide on measures to publicise their plight. They could write letters to the local papers and to MPs; draw pictures of the area that will be destroyed, prepare slogans, and design leaflets, posters, badges and car-stickers.

Those who welcome the reservoir might prepare a touring exhibition, describing and illustrating all the leisure activities that might take place on or around the new lake – angling, water-skiing, sailing, canoeing, subaqua diving, camping, caravanning, pony-trekking, bird-watching and so on. They could map the reservoir and surrounding area and show the location of picnic sites, an information centre, restaurant, mooring areas, sites for camping and caravanning, a ferry service etc. (It may well be interesting to consider that the 1,300 hectare reservoir, Rutland Water has been labelled a 'Special Protection Area' for birds under EC rules. It is now the winter home of 20,000 waterfowl.)

When all this information has been prepared and displayed for both sides to examine, hold a public inquiry, electing spokespeople to put across both points of view. Persuade someone to act as an inspector – the head, a school governor, the caretaker – and present him/her with the evidence so that a decision can be reached.

The children could write a report of the inquiry for the local paper, remembering to state the facts as they were presented, or draft an editorial giving their own views on the decision.

If a decision were made in favour of building a dam and reservoir, how would anyone who had to give up a home and land feel about it? They would be compensated of course, but how far would this help to soften the blow? Would they be able to take their protests further? What legal paths would still be open to them?

Shaker Lane, a picture book by Alice and Martin Provensen (Julia MacRae Books, 1987) concerns itself with the growth of a small community in the USA and the subsequent destruction of that community with the excavation of a reservoir and the construction of a dam. The book is well worth examining with older children in connection with work on the above project.

Again the arguments for and against the reservoir may be examined with reference to Shaker Lane and a meeting acted out between some of the residents and Ed Rikert, the County Land Agent.

If an inquiry were to be held about Shaker Lane, do children think that the results would have been any different?

Some children may go on to write about the excavation of the reservoir and the building of the dam in the form of a diary kept by Old Man Van Sloop. This might include details about the county purchase of the land, the dates when families move out and the beginning of work on the scheme. They could also record his thoughts about the new inhabitants of Shaker Lane – now called Reservoir Road.

Think about the submergence of a large area of land and how the scenery would be changed by this. Imagine diving in the reservoir and examining the newly-created underwater landscape. Point out that in times of severe drought, when water levels sink very low, some drowned villages have been partially uncovered revealing church spires and the roofs of houses. If children had been previously resident there, would this sight draw them back to look or would they prefer to keep away?

Drowned Valley

My happiness spawned and thrived
      in that valley,
My memories lie beneath forty
      fathoms of water,
The shop where I lived,
That claustrophobic, condensed
      room,
Now lies water-logged,
Uninhabited, desolate.
The musty dank atmosphere of
      the village church,
Is down there too.
Only the spire survives.

Daniel Benjamin Morden, 10 years (Form *Children as Writers 3*, Heinemann, 1976)

GLOBAL DEVELOPMENTS: THE THREAT TO TRIBAL SOCIETIES

Modern development threatens people in all parts of the globe and children should understand that the homes and livelihoods of many indigenous peoples are often at risk from encroaching development. People have lived in harmony with the rainforests for thousand of years. They take food from the forests and know which plants can provide life-saving medicines.

However, since the arrival of Columbus in the new world, scant regard has been paid to the survival of indigenous peoples. During the past five hundred years, the number of Indians in Brazil has fallen from nearly 9 million to less than 200,000 and many tribal groups now face the prospect of wholesale destruction brought about through the exploitation of their lands by 'civilised' man. The rights of the Aborigines in Australia have been ignored in favour of the profits to be made from tourism; oil exploitation is ruining land that once belonged to the Waorani of Ecuador, and many tribes have been devastated by epidemics of diseases brought in by outside settlers. Sometimes life becomes intolerable and people decide to leave their lands in search of better prospects elsewhere. Such 'environmental refugees' are growing in numbers, particularly in Africa.

Susan Jeffers takes inspiration for her picture book *Brother Eagle, Sister Sky*, (Hamish Hamilton, 1991) from the speech made by Chief Seattle in the mid 1850s when the government in Washington DC wanted to buy the lands of his defeated people:

> **We love this earth as a newborn baby loves it's mother's heartbeat.**
> **If we sell you our land, care for it as we have cared for it.**
> **Hold in your mind the memory of the land as it is when you received it.**
> **Preserve the land and the air and the rivers for your**
> **children's children and love it as we have loved it.**

It may well be useful to examine the plight of the North American Indians and to relate the loss of their lands to what is happening in other parts of the world today.

Jonathan Porritt writes of the lessons that we can learn from the natural world and how tribal people represent the solution to so many of the problems the world faces today: "Their survival is the key to our own survival. They are the best friends the Earth still has, and we should listen to them with as much care and attention as we can muster." (*Save the Earth*, Dorling Kindersley, 1991)

How do children feel about the ways in which indigenous people have been treated? Can anything be done at a local level? What can individuals do to promote an awareness of the problems?

The article below shows how the rock star Sting has campaigned to help save a huge area of the Brazilian rainforest for the tribal people who live there.

Sting saves rainforest

A CAMPAIGN by rock star Sting to save a huge area of Brazilian rainforest has been successful.

President Fernando Collor de Mello has agreed to give protected status to an area in the centre of Brazil two-thirds the size of Italy, the homeland of 2,000 Kayapo Indians.

This decision comes less than two weeks after the President gave protective designation to an area the size of Scotland for 10,000 Yanomani tribespeople in the northern Amazon.

Sting met the Kayapo chief during a trip to the Amazon in 1987. He was appalled by the effect uncontrolled logging and mining was having on the tribespeople.

He set up the Rainforest Foundation to help the Indians keep their lands, and to raise awareness of the consequences to native people of deforestation.

The foundation raised more than £580,000.

Brazil is hosting the Earth Summit on the environment next June.

Source: *Early Times*

The People Who Hugged the Trees is a classic Indian folktale adapted by Deborah Lee Rose (Robert Rinhart International, 1990). It tells the story of the first Chipko ('Hug-the-Tree') people who knew the importance of trees in their desert environment. The trees gave protection from sandstorms and shade from the sun. They signalled the presence of water in the desert. When the Maharajah ordered that the trees should be cut down because he needed wood for a fortress, the people hugged their trees and stood in the way of the axe-men. The Chipko movement is also active in India today where people are still trying to save their trees from big business enterprises.

Suggest that children examine the plight of tribal people in various parts of the world and bring their findings to the attention of their peers, school staff, governors and parents by means of a huge display and/or school assembly. Plan the project carefully and consider how different groups might address themselves to the various issues. One group might write letters to organisations asking for information and advice on how individuals may participate. (See addresses at the end of this chapter.) Another group might design posters, badges and car stickers with striking slogans that put across the message. Letters could also be written to MPs and to prominent spokespeople for the environment seeking their views. Lists could be drawn up detailing ways in which help may be offered to particular areas e.g. rainforests – don't buy items made from tropical timbers, don't buy exotic plants or birds if they were collected from the wild. Such advice should also include alternatives that may be bought.

Survival International, an organisation that campaigns for the rights of tribal people, suggests that one of the best ways to help is through the writing of letters to governments and companies who are harming them. The following is an example of how such a letter might be set out (this one is addressed to the President of Brazil) and is reproduced with the permission of Survival.

Exmo Fernando Collor de Mello
Presidente de la Republica
Palacio de Planalto
70.160 Brasilia DF
Brazil

Your address here
The date

Your Excellency

I was very upset to hear about the situation of the Yanomami Indians in Brazil. Miners are invading their land and polluting their rivers. The Indians are dying of malaria which they have caught from the goldminers and cannot get to the hospital which is very far away.

I respectfully ask you to help the Yanomami and to keep the goldminers off their land.

I look forward to hearing from you about this important matter.

Yours respectfully and sincerely

Children could also write form the point of view of someone whose lifestyle and home has been completely disrupted by inappropriate development. Poems might be written that follow a particular pattern, *Once we lived in.../but now we have only...; Once there were.../but now there's only...* etc. This might be written from the point of view of someone from a tribal society, or someone in this country who has lost his/her home through development. It could also be written from an animal's viewpoint (see 'Hare's Lament' in the chapter on Transport).

Adresses for Further Information

Department of the Environment, Publicity Stores, Building No 3, Victoria Road, South Ruislip, Middlesex HA4 0NZ
(Address for local plans leaflet mentioned in text.)

International Centre for Conservation Education, Greenfield House, Guiting Power, Gloucestershire GL54 5TZ

Native American Information Service, 21 Little Preston Street, Brighton BN1 2HQ
(Offers educational visits by speakers, storytelling workshops, plus a Native American Resource Pack for schools.)

Oxfam, 274 Banbury Road, Oxford OX2 7DZ

Survival International, 310 Edgware Road, London, W2 1DY
(Campaigns for the rights of tribal peoples – send 50p plus 50p postage for their 'Action Pack'.)

The Rainforest Foundation, 2 Ingate Place, Battersea, London SW8 3NS
(Brochures, broadsheets and 'Rainforests of the World' poster.)

World Development Movement, 25 Beehive Place, London SW9 7QR

READING RESOURCES

Poetry

Dancing Teepees – Poems of American Indian Youth, selected by Virginia Driving Hawk Sneve, with art by Stephen Gammell (OUP, 1989). A fascinating and illuminating selection.

Green Poetry selected by Robert Hull (Wayland, 1991) includes an extract from a speech made by Chief Seattle 'How can one sell the air?'.

The Last Rabbit edited by Jennifer Curry, (Methuen/Mammoth, 1990) includes 'The Chant of the Awakening Bulldozers' by Patricia Hubbell.

What on Earth...? Poems with a conservation theme, edited by Judith Nicholls (Faber, 1989) includes 'Countdown' by Judith Nicholls and 'The Day the Bulldozers Came' by David Orme.

Fiction

Adam's Common by David Wiseman (Corgi, 1989). The council are planning to build over Adam's Common. This is the story of one girl's attempts to stop the development from going ahead.

A Free Man on Sunday by Fay Sampson (Victor Gollancz, 1987). An account of the 1932 Mass Trespass on Kinder Scout in Derbyshire though the eyes of Edie Ramsden, daughter of one of the men who were imprisoned for believing in the freedom of individuals to walk the hills. Parallels can be drawn with what is happening in the countryside today.

Isn't it a Beautiful Meadow? by Wolf Harranth and Winifred Opgenoorth (OUP, 1990). Picture Book. Read in conjunction with the lines quoted above from Clare Bevan's *Mightier than the Sword*. At the end of the book the beautiful meadow is indistinguishable from the town that is left behind.

Never Walk Alone by Gareth Owen (Lions, 1991). Children try out various means to protest against the redevelopment of Grace Park, the place where they have always played football. Lots to discuss regarding the effectiveness of various courses of action.

The Farm That Ran Out Of Names by William Mayne (Red Fox, 1991). Owen Tudor and his family refuse to move when the Water Board inform them that their valley is to be the site of a new dam and reservoir. An ark is built and with their animals on board, the reservoir becomes a new home for the family.

The Magician's House Quartet by William Corlett (Red Fox, 1992). Book 3 of the quartet *The Tunnel Behind the Waterfall* sees developers planning to turn Golden Valley, an area of land on the Welsh borders, into an adventure park.

Wild by Rosalind Kerven (Blackie, 1991). Development of a tourist megacentre threatens the lives of thousands of wild creatures that inhabit a Scottish mountain. Children engage in a campaign to alert the public and save the mountain.

Non-Fiction

Rainforests by Dr Brian Knapp (Simon & Schuster Young Books, 1991). Comprehensive survey of the forest environment – weather, plants, creatures, plus damage that outsiders are doing to the forests. Last section asks, 'Is there a future?'.

Rainforest Destruction (Save Our Earth series) by Tony Hare (Franklin Watts, 1990). Well-presented and useful information about forest peoples, their medicines, food etc. Also examines the effects of deforestation and suggests what can be done.

Save the Earth by Jonathan Porritt (Dorling Kindersley, 1991). 'At every point *Save the Earth* distinguishes between irreversible environmental damage (which cannot be undone) and the damage that the Earth will still forgive us if we act soon enough to set things straight.' Excellent compendium of articles – teachers' reference.

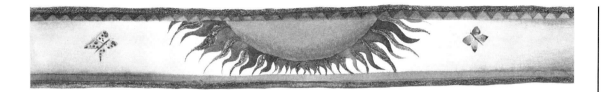

TRANSPORT

No one can deny that the huge growth in traffic on our roads presents a very serious problem. Suggest that children consider this problem and divide it up into different areas – pollution, noise, volume of traffic, accidents, new roads, etc.

POLLUTION

Some effects of pollution by cars are examined in the chapter on 'Atmospheric Pollution'. Children can now consider how these effects might be minimised. Posters could be designed which encourage people to cut down on inessential journeys. Others could promote the bicycle as a means of transport. However, there are disadvantages to riding a bicycle in busy city streets and these should be discussed. Children can think of ways in which our towns and cities might be made safer for bicycle users. Posters could also promote car sharing. In the morning trek to work, many cars have only one occupant but if two people were to share a car then there would be less pollution. The use of unleaded fuel could also be promoted. Can any fixtures be found that show how extensively it is now being used by motorists?

In pairs or groups, can children script a TV or radio advertisement to encourage either car sharing or switching to unleaded fuel? A number of factors will need to be taken into consideration – who is the target audience for the advertisement, when will be the best time of day to broadcast it, is there too much or too little language, will it give factual information, are points put over clearly, can it all be understood? It is important to remember that a TV or radio advertisement must last a certain number of seconds so that it can fill a time slot. How long will it last? If it is being made for TV, how much use will be made of visual language? If it is intended for radio, what sound effects or music will be required?

Once the advertisement is scripted, either record it on tape or 'perform' it to others in the way that you'd wish to see it on TV. How effective do the children find it? Would it encourage them to share a car or switch to unleaded fuel?

What about alternative energy sources for powering cars? Will these be developed and can they ever compete with petrol driven vehicles? List the various possibilities – batteries, solar power, alternative fuels such as methanol, ethanol and hydrogen, even animal dung! Design cars that might make use of these fuels.

NOISE

Noise can be a really worrying health problem to people living in cities or near main roads. Consider the effects of noise and how people adapt both their lifestyles and their properties to reduce noise levels. Vibrations from road traffic can also cause structural damage to buildings and road surfaces. Children could think of measures that might be adopted to help reduce noise levels from traffic. They could also produce a health and safety leaflet on noise pollution, explaining what it is, how it can damage health, and what can be done to alleviate it. Consider the language used to put across the various messages. Where would the leaflet be made available for people to pick up?

It might also be both interesting and revealing if children were able to make tape recordings of noise levels at various parts of their locality e.g. adjacent to a busy road, next to a railway track etc. Predict in advance the kind of sounds that will be heard and which will be the noisiest location. When the tape is replayed, ask children to list words that come to mind – clatter, crunch, rumble, rattle, chug, whine – then encourage them to write sound poems that make use of plenty of onomatopoeic words. Explore sound poems for different locations and record these onto tape:

Chug, chug, chug, chug,
clatterattle, clatterattle,
brrrrrrrrrrrrrrrrrrrrrrr
peep peep, honk honk,
squeeeeeeeeeeeeeeal.

VOLUME OF TRAFFIC

Consider how the volume of traffic can be reduced, particularly in city centres. What plans would children adopt to encourage cars to keep away? Such plans might include a total ban on cars from city centres. Cars would then be left on the outskirts and people would travel into the centre by public transport. More cycle routes could be provided to allow cyclists to travel in safety. An alternative proposal which would reduce volume of traffic by half each day would be to allow vehicles with even numbers on their number plates to enter the city centre on one day and odd numbers on another. (This has been tried out in Rome.) Are there other alternatives – tolls, a new public transport network etc.? Contact Transport 2000 (see address at the end of this chapter) and examine their proposals for reducing traffic in cities. Consider the advantages and disadvantages of their ideas. Children could then write a paragraph, or even produce a brochure outlining why they think that one of the proposals would be more successful than the others.

Are there problems with traffic around schools? If so this may be because the school is sited on a busy road, or it may only arise at the start and finish of the school day when parents drive up to collect children. Suggest that children carry out surveys at different times of the day to assess the volume of traffic that arrives and departs or passes by the school. Allow children to devise their own survey forms and to write up their findings. What can be learnt from surveying the same stretch of road at different times during the day? Are there too many cars around when school finishes? Do parents park sensibly? If there are problems, can children suggest what might be done to resolve them? Would their proposals work?

Many European cities have adopted 'traffic calming' procedures and some of these measures are being adopted in Britain. What do children understand by this? (Adding more bends to roads as they are built, adding traffic islands and speed bumps, reducing speed limits, making roads more narrow in places, particularly at crossroads, lining the road with trees etc.)

Suggest that children conduct interviews with local people to discover what is known about traffic calming and whether people think that such measures should be used more in this country. Can interviews be conducted with visitors from abroad who have personal experience of traffic calming measures? Children could write a report on their findings.

ACCIDENTS

What are the figures for the numbers of people killed or injured on British roads each year? How do these compare with other countries in Europe? Where are the accident 'black-spots' and what can be done about them? Can children produce a ten point charter for motorists which might help to cut down on accidents? Discuss <u>all</u> suggestions and then whittle them down to the ten most important ones. Produce as a poster that could be displayed around school. Similar posters could be designed for motorcyclists, cyclists and pedestrians.

NEW ROADS

As more and more roads are built so more of the countryside is lost. Also building more roads seems to encourage even more traffic as people are prepared to travel further to work. Has anyone ever travelled on a motorway such as the M25 during the morning's 'rush' to work? 'Rush' is in inverted commas because for much of the time traffic moves at a snail's pace or is even at a standstill. Adding another lane to the motorway, as is planned, will probably mean that it simply fills up with traffic again as soon as it is built. Discuss this problem and ask if children can think of possible solutions.

Emma and Sammy write a letter from the Earth in which our planet moans about the increase in traffic:

...I'm finding my life gets greyer everyday. Could you please tell me what to do about these rumbling tummy aches. I keep getting lorries rumbling over my stomach, especially round the motorway belt.

                       Yours pollutively,
                       Earth

Emma Warren and Sammy Thomas, 11 years

Letters of complaint could be written to the Department of Transport, from London or any other major city, complaining about the increase in traffic and suggesting measures that might be taken to curb it.

In groups children could discuss and then list the arguments for and against the building of a new road, perhaps a by-pass – it would provide improved access to the town that it is by-passing, it would help traffic flow and relieve congestion, it would improve safety and the environment for pedestrians. Problems might include damage to people's homes, splitting a community, development of supercentres with people no longer shopping locally, loss of land for farming, loss of wildlife, further pollution, an increase in road accidents etc. (The Department of Transport produce a booklet entitled *Transport and the Environment*. Children can write and request a copy of this from the address at the end of this chapter. The book outlines action that has been taken to preserve wildlife and plants, including the building of badger fencing along with tunnels for badgers and toads where they regularly cross roads.) The picture book by Charles Keeping, *Adam and Paradise Island*, (OUP, 1989) may be appropriate here.

Collect newspaper cuttings on such issues as the Twyford Down Cutting Scheme for the M3 Motorway near Winchester, which threatens to destroy two ancient monuments and two sites of scientific interest while crossing an area of outstanding natural beauty. Children could review the evidence for and against such a scheme and decide whether enough consideration is being given to the environment.

Children at Chilton CP School in Ramsgate were concerned that a proposed access road to Ramsgate Harbour would be passing very close to their school. They sought views on the existing road, uncovering concern over the following problems:

A	Volume of traffic	35%
B	Unsuitability of road	31%
C	Accidents	13%
D	Disturbance to neighbourhood	6%
E	Exhaust pollution	6%
F	Noise	6%
G	Others	3%

Children then wrote laments for the creatures that would lose their homes in the destruction of their habitat:

---

from **Hare's Lament**

... Now I can sense them,
They're not far away.
The diggers, the workers, come closer each day.

I shall look for somewhere new to stay,
To get away from the digging that ruins my day.

Lisa Butler

Are cars really man's best friends? Discuss the issue, perhaps as a formal debate with speakers for both sides, and then take a vote.

Read Ian Souter's poem. When have children experienced being stuck in traffic jams? Where and when do most jams develop? Suggest that children draw up lists of activities that travellers in cars can pursue when they are caught in jams. What can the driver do to help him remain calm?

Stuck Here Forever!

1st gear,
    2nd gear,
        3rd gear – NEVER,
Are we to be stuck in this traffic FOREVER?

With,
Cars slowing, traffic growing,
Bumpers nudging, hardly budging.
Stop – start, stop – start. NO OVERTAKING!
Stop – start, stop – start, CONTINUAL BRAKING!

1st gear,
> 2nd gear,
>> 3rd gear– NEVER,
Are we to be stuck in this traffic FOREVER?

With,
Babies crying, mothers sighing,
Drivers glaring, horns blaring.
HONK! HONK! HONK! PEEP! PEEP! PEEP!
CARS, CARS, CARS like SHEEP, SHEEP, SHEEP!

1st gear,
> 2nd gear,
>> 3rd gear – NEVER,
Are we to be stuck in this traffic FOREVER?

With,
Engines turning, fumes burning,
Petrol oxidising, pollution rising.
SMOKE! SMOKE! SMOKE! CHOKE! CHOKE! CHOKE!
A solution to pollution – a masterstroke.

1st hour,
> 2nd hour,
>> 3rd hour's gone.
I'LL BE ANOTHER YEAR OLDER BEFORE WE MOVE ON!

Ian Souter

Some children might like to write traffic jam poems of their own which might include a repeating line, as in the poem above. Try to capture the frustration of going nowhere fast!

Experiments in European cities such as Zurich and Heidelberg have proved that extensive tram or trolley-bus networks could help to reduce problems of traffic congestion. Zurich uses brightly coloured trolley buses that run frequently, regularly and where people want them to. The trolley bus is seen as being far more environmentally-friendly than the car, and people have begun to feel guilty about using their cars in the city.

Similar systems in Britain's cities might help although in country areas, where buses are non-existent or perhaps limited to just two days a week, cars will still be needed for most journeys. How would children attempt to improve public transport, bearing in mind that their budgets would be limited?

ALTERNATIVES TO ROAD TRANSPORT

There is a huge network of inland waterways in Britain, much of which is still navigable. This would provide an efficient and effective way of transporting goods if businesses could be encouraged to switch from road transport. Costs would be cheaper too. Ann Bonner's observations below, may promote discussion about whether canals could be a viable proposition today:

Canal

The road that bridges the canal thunders with the sound of lorries. Giant pantechnicons carry their cargo to the nearby motorway. Grit flies from gutters into eyes. Exhaust fumes puff at traffic lights on red.

Below the bridge the water lies stagnant, ochre-yellow. Empty bottles float. The rusty skeleton of a bike rears from murky depths.

Along the towpath tired elders and hawthorns are draped with tattered shreds of polythene, grey and black, blowing in the wind. Scrapyards, obscure small factories huddling haphazard, flank the dirty ribbon of water snaking into the distance.

No reclamation for the boating public here. No quiet fishermen cast lines into this liquid poison.

Only the thought, caught for a moment between the traffic's din, of the men who cut the Cut. Of the slow horses and long narrowboats hauling coal and iron. Of the families who lived on, and worked, this forlorn, forgotten waterway.

Ann Bonner

The particular place described above sounds rather unattractive. Ask children to pick out words and phrases that help to set the scene: "Grit flies from gutters into eyes", "Exhaust fumes puff", "water lies stagnant", "liquid poison" etc. Can children think of somewhere that they know, either nearby or a place that they have visited, that isn't a particularly pleasant place? If possible the place might have some connection with transport – a derelict railway station, the London Underground at night, a polluted river, a bus station on a rainy day – and then describe it in a similar way, detailing a number of unpleasant features. Then finally, as Ann Bonner has done, can they introduce something pleasant, perhaps a memory of past times when life was different, perhaps something unexpected, startling or even attractive?

The Underground

Down under the earth,
dirty, smelly, smoke-stained,
a maze of tunnels.
Old man drawing a last puff on a cigarette,
children yelling, mothers moaning,
rats scurry across the tracks
as a bright light appears out of the tunnel.

The platform is vacant and dark now,
all except for a cigarette end
glowing in emptiness.

Matthew Powell, 12 years

It might also be interesting to examine the poem by William Wordsworth "Composed Upon Westminster Bridge. September 3, 1802" and to talk about how different the view from the same bridge would be today, almost two hundred years since Wordsworth wrote.

AIR TRAVEL

There are two major problems with travelling by air. Planes consume huge amounts of fuel and make a lot of noise. They can also be caught in 'traffic jams' as they circle large airports, using up fuel and producing fumes. However new designs for more fuel efficient planes combined with regulations governing just how much nitrous oxide is emitted, may help to lessen the amount of greenhouse gases produced by aircraft.

What can children discover about the ways in which airports and airlines have attempted to reduce the levels of noise pollution suffered by people living within close proximity to Heathrow and Gatwick? Such findings will probably include reductions in the numbers of night flights, alternating runways for take-offs and landings, replacing older planes with quieter aircraft, and offering noise insulation grants. Consequently the number of people affected by noise pollution at Heathrow has dropped to a quarter of what it was fifteen or twenty years ago. Children should also consider what happens at destinations. Many flights are for package holidays and a huge increase in air traffic, along with the influx of visitors, must have a pronounced effect on local cultures and environment.

(The Department of Transport booklet *Transport and the Environment* mentioned above, contains a particularly useful section on noise pollution.)

RAIL TRAVEL

What are the advantages of travel by rail? Trains are efficient users of fuel when we consider how many passengers they carry and the number of miles they run. (More than 75% of all commuting into central London is by rail, more than in any other major European city.) With more and more trains being powered by electricity, railways should produce very little pollution in the future. New designs should also mean that trains travel much faster. A disadvantage for freight however, is that railways can't deliver from door-to-door although this may be overcome using transport by road at both ends of the journey. This may prove particularly suitable for international freight using the Channel Tunnel.

The construction of the Channel Tunnel itself has had a huge impact on the local environment, although Eurotunnel have attempted to minimise this through the development and maintenance of an extensive environmental policy. Suggest that children write to Eurotunnel (address below) and request information on how their policy has been implemented. Aerial photographs of the Folkestone Terminal could be displayed, and children asked to discuss and then list the various environmental problems that would have resulted from such a change in the landscape. Such lists might include re-location of animal habitats, re-planting of displaced vegetation, dismantling and re-building of listed buildings, archaeological rescue work, the adoption of noise insulation measures similar to those taken at airports, monitoring day-to-day working practices to minimise adverse effects on the local community etc.

Addresses for Further Information

Campaign for Lead-Free Air (CLEAR), 3 Endsleigh Street, London WC1H 0DD

Council for the Protection of Rural England, Warwick House, 25 Buckingham Palace Road, London SW1W 0PP

Department of Transport, 2 Marsham Street, London SW1P 3EB

Eurotunnel Exhibition Centre, St Martin's Plain, Cheriton High Street, Folkestone, Kent CT19 4QD

Open Spaces Society, 25a Bell street, Henley-on-Thames, Oxon RG9 2BA

Pedestrians' Association, 1 Wandsworth Road, London SW8 2WX

Transport 2000, Walkden House, 10 Melton Street, London NW1 2EJ

Reading Resources

Poetry

A Fourth Poetry Book compiled by John Foster (OUP, 1982) includes 'The Narrow Boats' by Gregory Harrison, 'Car Dump' by Alan Silitoe and 'The Country Bus' by Gwen Dunn.

Autogeddon by Heathcote Williams (Cape, 1991). A clever and powerful examination in verse of the centrality of cars in the world today. Plenty to interest. Adult book but carefully selected extracts would encourage much discussion as to how we view cars.

The Green Umbrella, stories, songs, poems and starting points for environmental assemblies compiled by Jill Brand (A & C Black, 1991). Includes 'This is the bike...' and 'Man's best friend' by Trevor Millum, and 'Person-power' by John Rice.

What on Earth...? Poems with a Conservation Theme, edited by Judith Nicholls (Faber, 1989) includes 'Sonic Boom' by John Updike.

Non-Fiction

A Green Perspective – Eurotunnel and the Environment (Eurotunnel, 1991). A photographic record of the various ways in which Eurotunnel have paid attention to environmental concerns. Available from Eurotunnel Exhibition Centre.

Channel Tunnel by Lionel Bender (Franklin Watts, 1990). Covers planning of the tunnel, how the route was chosen, boring from England and France, the terminals, safety aspects etc. Also in same 'Young Engineer' series, *Airliner* and *Supercar*.

Traffic Pollution by M Bright (Franklin Watts, 1991). Good survey of the various problems caused by traffic pollution – noise, exhaust gases, smog, threats to health – plus alternatives to petrol.

ATMOSPHERIC POLLUTION

How do we know that air is dirty? Sometimes we can see it – smoke from factory chimneys, exhausts, bonfires, and cigarettes. If we touch smooth surfaces such as cars or windows, our fingers are blackened by dirt that is deposited. Ask children to list the various ways in which air is polluted. What about pollution we can't see? Alternatively, take children into the school playground or a busy street and ask them to note down all the ways in which air is being polluted.

The burning of fossil fuels such as coal, coke and oil is one of the most serious causes of air pollution in industrialised countries, resulting in the production of smoke, sulphur-dioxide and dust. The Great London Smogs of the early 1950s resulted in the introduction of the first Clean Air Act in 1956. Suggest that children research smog and discover why it proved so dangerous to health. Alan Collinson in his book *Pollution* (Cloverleaf/Evans Brothers, 1991) writes about his own experiences in the worst London smog of December 1952.

Many children may have seen dramatic pictures in the newspapers prior to Christmas 1991 when smog conditions appeared to have returned to London. In this instance high levels of nitrogen-dioxide from car exhaust fumes became trapped on the ground in stagnant air, reaching levels that equalled those in Los Angeles where smog is a regular occurrence. Again, health warnings were issued advising that babies, the elderly and anyone with respiratory problems shouldn't go out into busy car-filled streets.

Suggest that some children might write to newspapers and magazines outlining their worries about air pollution, as Megan Fisher did when she contacted *Early Times*:

I'm writing on a subject I feel very strongly about - air pollution.

Although it is something that frequently pops up in the newspapers, there are some people who suffer a lot more than others without realising it.

Some of those are asthmatics, like myself. I go to boarding school in Sussex and my home is in Essex, close to the industrial area, Canvey Island.

Every time I go home for the holidays, I immediately notice my chest becoming tight and wheezy – it's not the house dust, it's the chemicals in the air! Back at school I'm fine – because there are no dangerous chemicals in the air. I hope other people, especially chest disease sufferers, like asthmatics will realise how badly the chemicals in the atmosphere are affecting the nation's health.

There is no need for it all – something must be done, and it is up to US to persuade the Government to take action, quickly!

Megan Fisher

What do children already know about 'The Greenhouse Effect'? What is it and what are its effects? Ensure that they understand that two naturally occurring greenhouse gases – carbon-dioxide and water vapour – are necessary, as without them the Earth would be about 30 degrees cooler than it is today. However, by adding to these gases through the burning of fossil fuels, car and lorry exhaust emissions, forest clearance and so on, we run the risk of overheating the Earth as carbon-dioxide acts as an insulator and reflects back heat from the earth that would normally be passed back to space. A further pollutant gas, methane, is 25 times more capable of retaining heat than carbon-dioxide. Children could research this to discover where it is produced – rotting vegetation, buried rubbish, wet swampy paddy fields, leakages from coal mines and natural gas pipes. Set them to discover why the destruction of rainforests allied with the increase in grazing land for cattle are factors helping to fuel the greenhouse effect. (Answer: Methane is produced in the intestines of cattle and on average each cow releases 22 grams of methane from its bowels every day!)

Many scientists believe that as the earth warms up, ice melting in Greenland and the Antarctic will cause a rise in sea levels by as much as 20 to 40 cm. Other scientists believe that the rise in temperature will be much smaller than predicted and far more gradual. A Meteorological Office report, published in January 1992, claims that previous forecasts have substantially underestimated the oceans' capacity to absorb heat and slow down the damage caused by pollutants trapping warmth in the atmosphere. Nevertheless, there is no denying that global warming is definitely with us. Seven of the eight hottest years in the past century occurred between 1980 and 1987 and our world in the 1990s is almost two degrees higher than that of the 1880s.

A useful review of the greenhouse effect may be found in *The Blue Peter Green Book* by Lewis Bronze, Nick Heathcote and Peter Brown (BBC/Sainsbury's, 1990). Pictorially, a section of Earth is contained within a greenhouse and surrounded by informative annotations.

Children can discuss and then list the probable effects of global warming – ice caps melting along with glaciers on mountains, a rise in sea level which could have disastrous results for islands or low lying countries such as the Netherlands, changing climate bringing an increase in natural disasters such as hurricanes, floods and drought.

Ann Bonner writes of small yet significant changes in weather and climate which makes the month of December seem somehow different to how she remembers it from childhood. Are these the really noticeable results of global warming for the individual?

December!

In memory a month of childhood Christmases when stars shone brilliant in winter skies. Of blood red teatime sunsets, and the creeping cold onset of night.

Mornings brought hoarfrost, ice-bound puddles, frozen ponds. If we were lucky, snow.

Today is first Sunday in Advent. And first day of December. Church bells ring. The morning is mild. A damp mist clings to trees that still hold their leaves, dotted gold on birches and hawthorns, stubborn bronze on oaks. Will they be there at Christmas? The curled yellow leaves of the flowering cherry lie fresh-fallen on emerald grass. Daffodil bulbs, planted in autumn, show green tips in the soft, black soil.

Is this December? Are overcoats redundant? Will 'White Christmas' be the stuff of legend? Where, oh where, is winter?

Only there, on the Christmas card.

Ann Bonner

Suggest that children write as if it were some way in the future. Imagine that they are looking back on changes in weather patterns, perhaps more dramatic changes than those mentioned in the above piece. Alternatively, changes may be implied as in Nick's piece where he repeats the phrase "I remember...":

I Remember...

I remember what it was like
to swim in safe seas,
to breathe clean air
and to see animals.
I remember what it was like
to see hills and hills
of lovely green grass,
to see a rainbow
and not to be boiling hot
every second of the day.
I remember what it was like.

Nick Kemp, 10 years

Suggest that children collect cuttings about global warming. What predictions are being made for the future? Can children write their own newspaper articles as if they were writing from some point in the future? These could describe a marvellous new invention that helped to solve the problem or, alternatively, describe a disaster such as the flooding of low-lying towns or villages, something that is predicted in many of the present day 'prophecies of doom'.

In their lists of air pollutants, some children may have included CFCs (Chlorofluorocarbons) – the propellant gasses for aerosols – and they may be aware that these are doubly dangerous, as a greenhouse gas and also through their creation of a hole in the ozone layer. ('Hole' is probably the wrong word as the problem develops when the ozone layer wears thin.) Check that children are aware that ozone gas stops ultraviolet light – a dangerous kind of sunlight – from reaching the Earth where it could harm us. Can children research how scientists first discovered the damage to the ozone layer over the North and South Poles each spring? (The largest so-called hole is over the Antarctic and is thought to be as big as the USA.)

What is known about other items where CFCs are found – foam packaging, fast-food containers, coolants from fridges and air conditioners, padding from cushions and cars? Although the quantity of CFC gas in the atmosphere is quite small, it is over 10,000 times more effective at trapping heat than carbon-dioxide.

Suggest that children survey their own homes to discover which of the aerosols in regular use are 'ozone-friendly'. Many companies now state this on the can. If it isn't marked, suggest that children note down the address of the company producing the spray and then write to ask whether their products are ozone friendly. Suggest too, that children mount a publicity campaign around their school to make others aware of the necessity to think carefully about which spray cans are purchased. This could be carried out in groups to see which group can mount the most effective campaign. This could either be through the design of posters or by means of a mock radio or TV programme. Some children may enjoy composing slogans or even limericks:

> The new aerosol spray that we buy
> Can make terrible holes in the sky,
> So read every label
> And we should be able
> To lead better lives if we try.
>
> **Charles Romito,** 8 years

> A little green man from Outer Space
> Came to earth with a frown on his face,
> He said, 'Will you stop spraying,
> For the ozone's decaying
> And we don't want your junk in our place.'
>
> **Kate Ashton,** 8 years

Some scientists now believe that many of our so-called 'green' chemical substitutes for CFCs (Hydrochlorofluorocarbons, HCFCs) are still dangerous. Although not so damaging in their effects on the ozone layer, they will still be contributing to global warming in a big way because of the huge amounts that are now being released. It may be worth discussing this with children and considering whether anyone is ever really right when it comes to scientific speculation.

Suggest that children discuss and then try to list the various measures that should be taken to reduce global warming and ozone depletion. These may include – burning less fossil fuels, developing and making use of alternative energy sources, stopping tree felling and the burning of forests, planting new trees (they take up carbon-dioxide and prevent it reaching the atmosphere), developing substitutes for petrol, replacing CFCs with less damaging chemicals. (In countries such as China and India, fridges and air conditioning are new to most homes and the CFC problem could get much worse unless new chemicals can be introduced which are kinder to the ozone.)

In his book *Global Warming*, (Hodder & Stoughton, 1990), Lawrence Pringle reviews the various measures that should be taken to reduce greenhouse gases, but then warns that such a reduction will require co-operation between nations on a scale that has previously proved impossible. Pringle observes that unless the industrialised nations can assist Third World countries in the development of alternative energy sources that reduce emissions of carbon dioxide, then we are heading towards a bleak future.

Acid Rain

What do children understand about the term 'acid rain'? At its simplest, rain is being 'poisoned' by pollutants in the air. This pollution is emitted by road vehicles, homes, factories and power stations in the form of sulphur dioxide, nitrogen oxides, and hydrocarbons. Polluted rain was first recognised in the mid 19th century but between the 1950s and 1970s, acidity of the rain over Europe increased tenfold. There are some natural sources of air pollution – can children think what these might be? (volcanoes, swamps, rotting plants) but these have minimal effect compared with man-made pollution.

Ensure that children are aware that acid rain is a world-wide problem. More sulphur dioxide is produced by power stations in the UK than in any other EC country. Much of this pollution is carried on westerly winds to Scandinavia, Holland, Belgium and Germany where it causes considerable environmental damage.

In groups children could consider the effects of acid rain with regard to forests, lakes and rivers, and buildings. What do they think is happening and how extensive do they believe the problem to be?

Forests

Trees are dying before they can grow large enough to be cut for timber; in 1984, in what was then West Germany, 50% of trees were found to be damaged. Trees need good soil to grow in and acid rain damages the balance of different substances that make up the soil. Trees are then less healthy and easily harmed by viruses, fungi and insect pests.

Lakes and rivers

Levels of acidity in some Scandinavian lakes have increased by 100 times in just two or three years. Many of these are now totally empty of fish. When the snow melts in spring, acidity is highest in lakes and rivers. This is the time that fish breed and if the water is too acid then young fish will die.

Buildings

Acid rain destroys buildings and statues by eating into metal and stone. The stonework of St Paul's Cathedral is being eaten away by acid rain. Also many other world famous monuments such as Cologne Cathedral, Notre Dame, the Taj Mahal, the Parthenon and The Statue of Liberty have suffered from extensive corrosion. John Foster's poem points to a bleak future:

Graveyard Scene

There are no names on the gravestones now,
They've been washed away by the rain.
The graveyard trees are skeletons now,
They will never wear leaves again.

Instead of a forest, the tower surveys
A bleak and desolate plain.
Those are not tears in the gargoyle's eyes,
They are droplets of acid rain.

John Foster

Once the problems have been identified, further discussion can take place concerning measures that might prove beneficial. Some progress has already been made but there is much more that needs to be done. Since vehicle exhaust fumes are one of the main causes of air pollution, it is now recognised that cars need to be fitted with catalytic converters which convert the harmful exhaust gases into carbon dioxide, nitrogen and water. In Germany nearly half of all new cars are now fitted with converters and the EC has agreed that they will be fitted to all new small cars from 1992.

Restricting the use of private motor vehicles would also help to cut down harmful emissions. Children might care to consider how this might be done. Should the cost of owning and running a car be increased or should cars be banned from city centres? What about developing countries where the demand for cars is great?

Measures to reduce sulphur dioxide pollution from factories and power stations are expensive to set up and run, but it is possible to remove the sulphur from coal before it is burnt or to fit special cleaning devices to chimneys. Electricity can also be generated from forms of energy that don't produce acid rain. (These are examined elsewhere.)

Some lakes in Scandinavia are slowly being cleaned up but it will take many years and a high degree of international co-operation on pollution control before there are significant and long lasting improvements.

Can children think of measures that might be taken at a local level? These could include turning off lights when they are not needed so that power stations do not have to generate so much electricity; cutting back on car use – walk to school(!); making others aware of the problem through a poster campaign or school assembly; writing letters to point out the problem and to indicate what measures might be taken. In the example below, Michelle writes to the Prime Minister at the time, Margaret Thatcher. This could be read to children who wish to pen letters of their own. Discuss the way that the letter is written. Point out that it is courteous in tone and well thought out. Note also how Michelle lets Mrs Thatcher know that she has studied the problem, is knowledgeable about it and has formed her own opinions.

Mrs Thatcher
10 Downing Street
London

Dear Mrs Thatcher

I am very worried about what is happening to our environment because of acid rain.

I am very sad to see the things that are happening in many countries in Europe and around the world. Fish and trees dying, lakes needing to be limed as they are too acidic.

I know that acid rain is produced by sulphur and nitrogen gases produced by power stations, many of which are in Britain, and was wondering what your government are doing to combat this great problem?

Recently, in one of my geography lessons at school, I saw some figures of how many tonnes of sulphur dioxide a year is estimated to be produced by each country in Europe. My friends and I were ashamed at the very high number of tonnes in Britain, around six million tonnes.

Is there nothing we can do to stop this terrible problem?

... We are destroying our world for the generations to follow us. Do you not think it is about time we did something about it?

Yours sincerely

Michelle Millar

Addresses for Further Information

Acid Rain Information Centre, Department of Environment and Geography, Manchester Polytechnic, John Dalton Extension, Chester Street, Manchester M1 5GD

Campaign for Lead-Free Air (CLEAR), 3 Endsleigh Street, London WC1H 0DD

Friends of the Earth, 26 - 28 Underwood Street, London N1 7JQ

National Society for Clean Air, 136 North Street, Brighton, East Sussex BN1 1RG

WATCH Trust for Environmental Education, 22 The Green, Nettleham, Lincoln LN2 2NR

Reading Resources

Poetry

The Last Rabbit – A Collection of Green Poems, edited by Jennifer Curry (Methuen/Mammoth, 1990) includes 'Coal Black – Grass Green' by Jennifer Curry.

What on Earth...? Poems with a Conservation Theme, edited by Judith Nicholls (Faber, 1989). Contains 'Chill, burning rain' by John Kitching and 'Poisoned Talk' by Raymond Wilson.

Non-Fiction

Acid Rain by Stephen Sterline (Wayland, 1991). A particularly clear text for the younger end of the age range. Examines how rain becomes acid and its effects on the environment. Well illustrated.

Acid Rain by Tony Hare (Franklin Watts, 1990). Another worthwhile volume in the 'Save Our Earth' series. Clear text and striking photography. Covers dead lakes, damage to trees, soil and buildings, plus suggestions as to what might be done.

Air by Steve Pollock and Peter Wingham (Belitha Press, 1990). Good introduction to the various ways in which air is being polluted.

The Greenhouse Effect and *Acid Rain*, both books by M Bright (Franklin Watts, 1991). Excellent for the younger age range. Clear explanations of both phenomena, plus effects and possible solutions.

The Greenhouse Effect by Tony Hare (Franklin Watts, 1990). An excellent survey of the culprits and a review of the evidence. Suggestions as to what can be done to reverse the threat.

The Junior Guide to Air Pollution and *An Introduction to Pollution*, both produced by the National Society for Clean Air and Environmental Protection. (See address above.) Single copies of the former are free, the latter costs £3.00. Many free factsheets.

This Fragile Earth by John Baines and Barbara James (Simon & Schuster, 1991). A comprehensive review of major issues including the greenhouse effect, the ozone layer and acid rain. Clear and informative illustrations.

Too Hot to Handle? The Greenhouse Effect by Mary Gribbin with John Gribben (Corgi, 1992). Causes of the greenhouse effect are examined along with its implications for the world. Surveys ways in which governments and individuals can help nature to cope with the build-up of greenhouse gases.

ENERGY DEMANDS
....

Discover what children understand by energy. The food we eat gives us energy and we need it to stay alive. Energy in some form needs to be supplied to machines before they can work. Almost all the energy we use originally came from the sun. It is stored in food, in the plants we eat and in the animals that have fed on plants. It is also stored in fossil fuels. Can children list these and find out how they came to be in the earth?

Can children think of ways in which energy in the form of coal, gas, oil, electricity etc has transformed our lives. Think particularly of the benefits that they have brought us.

Ask children to identify other sources of energy that we make use of today. A list of such sources might include – nuclear power, hydro-electricity, tidal, solar and wind power and turf burning. Children could bring to school and display examples of items that make use of particular sources of energy – something powered by batteries, a solar powered calculator, an oil lamp, a light bulb, calor gas stove with an empty canister, a toy windmill etc. The various areas can then be researched under headings – history, present uses, advantages, disadvantages.

It is important that children understand the difference between renewable and non-renewable sources of energy. Just as our own energy can run out if we don't replace it through eating, so fossil fuels are finite too and may well run out within the next one hundred years. Discuss also, the fact that developing countries use far less non-renewable resources than developed countries, relying instead on wood, animal dung and animal power for the energy they use in farming, heating and cooking.

How does our use of energy affect the environment? Children can brainstorm group lists and then try to agree a joint one. Such a list might include: unsightly evidence of fuel extraction such as spoil heaps; increasing threat of global warming; acid rain; smog; accidental damage to wildlife habitats such as oil spills and contamination of rivers and streams; risk of nuclear accidents, and other danger to human life, for example oil rig fires and leakages from chemical plants.

Environmental disasters such as oil spills or chemical leakages have become all too common in recent years. Topical stories could be examined by children and then re-written for class newspapers. Alternatively, a fictitious disaster might be agreed upon and then commented on in various ways – a news report for radio or television, a letter from someone caught up in the events, a newspaper account or editorial, diary entries that show the progress of attempts to halt the disaster, interviews with people in the know etc. In the news report below, Yaron writes about an oil spill and includes a comment from the captain of the stricken ship along with speculation from the environmental group, Friends of the Earth.

THE TELEGRAPH

OIL TANKER HOLED ON ROCKS, BEACHES UNDER THREAT.

A Saudi Arabian tanker failed to reach Norway when it was holed on rocks. The oil is poring out in gallons. There are rescue teams trying to get the crew out. The tanker carries 80,000 gallons of crude oil. Scientists are already on their way to the crisis.

The crisis began on July 6th when the tanker hit rocks on the West coast of France. Most of the oil has already seeped out into the sea. Experts say that if the world doesn't put a stop to the slick, it will carry on into Britain.

The forty year old captain, Philip Downing, lives in Riyadh, the capital of Saudi Arabia. He gives an eye-witness account: We were really close to the rocks before we saw them and then we couldn't change course in time. Before we knew it we were hit. I radioed France and Saudi Arabia and told them what had happened. In one hour a rescue team had come with a boom, ships, and scientists.

The RSPCA are arriving at the crisis to try to help the animals. Thousands of sea birds are being trapped by the oil.

The boom's captain says that the oil slick is too big to be caught in one go, so they will take a chance and separate the oil. Some governments don't approve of the idea because the oil might flow in different ways right round the Earth.

Environmental groups are thinking of ideas to stop oil slicks once and for all. Some ideas are already in action. Friends of the Earth say:

We are designing a new kind of transport for oil. It is a submarine which can carry as much oil as a tanker and can go just as fast. If it has a leak an alarm will sound. The captain has a remote control to get the sub to safety. The iron and steel walls prevent the oil from escaping into the sea. A hose will suck the oil into special emergency oil drums.

Reported by Yaron Simpson

What do children know already about the devastating effects that oil spills can have on wildlife? What emergency measures do the oil industry bring into operation when a spill takes place? Yaron mentions the use of booms in his report, but can children discover any other ways of controlling the spread of oil, or cleaning it up?

The oil wells set ablaze during the Gulf War in early 1991 show that sources of fuel can be vulnerable. The nuclear industry point to this as an argument for diversity of fuels within any one country so that any threats to its energy supply, whether through war, industrial unrest or freak weather can be minimised. The industry claims that its use in Britain saves the equivalent of 100 million barrels of oil each year.

A striking picture book by Graham Oakley, *Henry's Quest* (Macmillan Children's Books, 1986) shows the possible results of placing too much dependence on one particular fuel, in this instance, petrol. Society has returned to Medievalism and pictures show an overgrown chemical plant, pylons functioning as lookout towers, an airliner with thatched porches and piles of discarded electrical equipment. Henry's quest is to find petrol to power the king's heirlooms – a fleet of limousines. Whoever finds petrol will also be able to claim the king's daughter as his bride. After a series of adventures through decayed and corrupt urban life, Henry returns with the petrol. The book cannot fail to promote speculative discussion at all levels.

This might be a good point at which to consider nuclear power and its implications. Children should realise that because fossil fuels will one day be used up, scientists saw the possibility of nuclear power as an attractive replacement. Today, however, it is increasingly evident that nuclear power is not such a cheap and abundant source of energy as was once thought. Figures now indicate that only 6% of the UK's energy and 4% of the world's comes from nuclear power.

What do children already know about the contentious issues that surround the nuclear industry? They will probably be aware that the disposal of radioactive waste poses a mammoth problem which is only partially solved by burying it deep in the earth. There is also the health risk to workers, the public and the environment, and people are far more aware of this since the Chernobyl disaster in 1986. (*The Chernobyl Catastrophe* by Graham Pickard, published by Wayland, 1988 gives a very good insight into what actually happened and the subsequent extent of the contamination.)

Children may already have fixed views about the nuclear industry particularly if they live in areas close to nuclear power stations. However, both sides of the argument should be explored and the issue debated. British Nuclear Fuels plc provide a range of services for schools (see address below), and an examination of some of their publications will allow children to discover reasons why nuclear power is still viewed by some people as the best long-term replacement for fossil fuels.

Nuclear power stations, for example, do not help create acid rain or produce carbon dioxide, a major contribution to the greenhouse effect.

Once the issue has been examined, children should be able to draw up a balance sheet of advantages and disadvantages covering such areas as safety, pollution, disposal of waste etc. They can then indicate whether their own views have shifted at all whilst they have been carrying out their research. (Similar balance sheets could also be drawn up regarding other sources of energy, all of which have some sort of impact on the environment.)

For older children there are several works of fiction concerned with aspects of the nuclear age and mature readers of twelve or above way wish to try one of these books (see reading resources).

Robins Mellor's powerful poem lends itself to much discussion. Read the poem twice and then ask for comments.

The Dragons Are Almost Here

I wandered to an empty place
& in the sun I lay,
but many fearful dragons came
with eyes of gold & tongues of flame,
bringing darkness to the day.
The dragon of black, poisoned breath
spoke with a hissing sound,
"I'll spit out fumes & deadly gasses,
wither trees & burn the grasses
& leave bare, empty ground."

The dragon of oil & foam & scum
spoke like slippery snow,
"I'll kill the rivers & the seas,
I'll spread thick slime & wet disease
in every place I go."

> A dragon, then stepped from the crowd,
> her face was a crystal flame,
> "I have a place for you," she said,
> I stumbled back & shook my head,
> she beckoned me to join the dead,
> radiation was her name.
>
> They are coming soon to every place,
> they are coming very near;
> I see flowers die & forests burn,
> I hear their voices at every turn,
> the dragons are almost here.
>
> **Robin Mellor**

Why has the poet chosen dragons to symbolise the various threats that beset us? It is a particularly bleak poem with no hint of salvation, is it too bleak a picture?

Could something similar be written from a more optimistic perspective, perhaps looking back from a hundred years into the future, recalling how the dragons were vanquished. The poem might have a similar structure:

> The dragon of black, poisoned breath
> spoke with a hissing sound,
> but solar, wind and tidal power
> destroyed that dragon's finest hour
> and laid her in the ground.

Children might like to read the poem aloud and to decide how the different dragons might speak. One speaks "... with a hissing sound" and another "... like slippery snow". What kind of voice would fit the dragon called 'Radiation'?

It will be useful perhaps, to examine ways in which the power industry is now paying attention to environmental considerations. The nuclear industry is endeavouring to promote a commitment to the environment. Nature reserves are being developed around a number of power stations and there are trails that school parties may follow. Children might care to write for details (see address below).

British Coal Opencast mine coal from shallow deposits using earthmoving machinery. The land is then restored for agricultural, leisure or wildlife use. In all production contracts there are at least 35 different clauses dealing with the environment, and before any mining begins, a survey establishes areas of specialist wildlife interest that may need protection or removal to a new location. (No one knows however, whether relocation of a species will be successful.) Special projects are being set up by British Coal Opencast to investigate how badger setts can be safeguarded. On many occasions it proves possible for setts to remain in place during open-casting although at other times setts may be re-located into new territories where they will find sympathetic landowners.

Children may like to write to British Coal Opencast and ask for copies of their publications dealing with badgers (see address below).

A different view of opencast operations may be obtained through reading *Dragline* by Susan Gates (Oxford University Press, 1991). Although this novel is really for teenage readers, selected extracts might well be read to younger children as it focuses on the problems of living in close proximity to the noise and pollution of opencast mining.

There are no quick and easy answers when it comes to finding cost-effective sources of energy to replace fossil fuels or nuclear power. What do children know about renewable energy sources – wind, solar, tidal, geothermal, hydroelectric power, even rubbish burning. Groups could research the different areas to discover advantages and disadvantages. For example, solar power is clean and silent but is only available in daylight hours and varies according to weather and season. Wind power is strongest in the winter when most power is required but the large turbines are very noisy and look rather unsightly when they are built in remote areas.

A Gallup poll, commissioned by Friends of the Earth, recorded that 87% of people thought that the Government should be doing more to develop renewable energy projects, and of this figure more than 75% were prepared to pay more for renewable energy. FoE also state that several international bodies have recently estimated that the potential amount of energy we could harness from such technologies would be greater than the current total energy use in the world. Proper investment could lead to Britain taking 20% of its energy from renewable sources by the year 2020.

A class letter seeking information about renewable energy projects might be composed and sent to the Centre for Alternative Technology in Wales (see address below).

If energy is to be conserved and environmental threats tackled, then energy demands will need to be greatly reduced and energy efficiency improved. Children can consider how individuals can take action through an examination of energy efficiency in their homes. Think of how houses can be designed so that they use less energy. Children may care to draw pictures of houses which exhibit energy saving features. The pictures can then be annotated. Some of the features included could be loft insulation, cavity wall and floor insulation, thermostats on radiators, double glazing, lagged hot water tank, time switches, solar panels, shower, energy saving light bulbs etc. Suggestions could be arrived at for saving energy in the home, for example turning off unnecessary lights, turning down the thermostat and installing some of the features mentioned above.

Bring in a collection of reports on houses for sale from estate agents. Ask children to look carefully at how each house is advertised and note any energy saving features that are mentioned. Which would be the most energy efficient buy? Children might like to prepare similar reports about the houses that they have designed, stressing the various features that they have incorporated.

A similar examination could be made into energy efficiency at school. Are lights left on for prolonged periods when rooms are not in use? Where is heat lost through outside doors being left open? Is the school boiler insulated? Heat plans of the school could be drawn up showing hot and cold spots, the warmest rooms, draughty areas and so on. Findings could then be relayed to the rest of the school at an assembly and posters produced to encourage children to think about energy conservation within the school.

Some children might like to produce storyboards which show the choices that we can make when trying to reduce energy consumption in the home or at school. These could show what happens during the day and how individual choice affects energy levels. The first boxes might read: 1. Cold morning/Turn up thermostat on heating or wear a thicker jumper? 2. Toast for breakfast/Switch on large oven grill or pop bread in toaster? 3. Time for school/Ask dad or mum to get the car out or take a brisk walk? Activities such as this will help to reinforce the message that individuals can make a difference. By changing our behaviour and cutting our energy use, we can help reduce the energy crisis.

Addresses for Further Information

British Coal Opencast, 200 Lichfield Road, Mansfield, Notts NG18 4RG

British Coal Schools Service, Public Relations Department, Room 339, Hobart House, Grosvenor Place, London SW1X 7AE

British Gas Education Services, PO Box 46, Hounslow, Middlesex TW4 6NF

British Nuclear Fuels plc, Corporate Education Unit, Dalton House, Risley, Warrington, Cheshire WA3 6AS

Consumers Against Nuclear Energy, PO Box 697, London NW1 8YQ

Department of Energy, Thames House South, Millbank, London SW1P 4QJ

National Centre for Alternative Technology, Llwyngwern Quarry, Machynlleth, Powys, SY20 9AZ

Neighbourhood Energy Action, 2/4 Bigg Market, Newcastle-upon-Tyne NE1 1WW

National Power, Senator House, 85 Queen Victoria Street, London EC4 4DP

NIREX Information Centre, Curie Avenue, Harwell, Didcot, Oxon OX11 0RH

Powergen Plc, Haslucks Green Road, Shirley, Solihull, West Midlands B90 4PD

The Electricity Council, 30 Millbank, London SW1P 4RD

The Solar Energy Society, Kings College London, Atkins Building South, 128 Campden Hill Road, London W8 7AH

Reading Resources

Poetry

What on Earth...? Poems with a Conservation Theme, edited by Judith Nicholls (Faber, 1989) includes 'Windscale' by Norman Nicholson.

Fiction

Brother in the Land by Robert Swindells (Puffin Plus, 1985), *Empty World* by John Christopher (Puffin Plus, 1981), and *Z for Zachariah* by Robert O'Brien (Lions Tracks, 1976). Three novels that deal with various aspects of life after a nuclear holocaust.

Goggle-Eyes by Anne Fine (Puffin, 1990). A sub-plot deals with a campaign of protest against a nuclear base. Excellent read.

Monster in Our Midst by Peggy Woodford (Macmillan Limelight, 1988). Alan and his friend Nick live in the shadow of Stagwell Nuclear Power Station. When Stagwell is announced as a site for the dumping of nuclear waste, both boys become involved in the campaign to prevent it happening.

(All these novels are too old for the age group but mature readers may wish to try one.)

Non-fiction

Energy Demands by Brian Gardiner (Franklin Watts, 1990). Examines the world's energy needs – finite fuels and sustainable fuels, plus energy conservation.

Environmentally Yours – A Green Handbook for Young People, (*Early Times*/Puffin, 1991). Good review of alternative energy sources.

Future Sources of Energy by Mark Lambert (Wayland, 1986). A well-illustrated survey of the various sources of renewable energy – sun, earth, air, water, wave, along with the place of the nuclear industry.

Junior Projects no. 50 'Energy' (Scholastic, 1990).

My World no. 8 'Energy' (Scholastic/WWF, 1991).

Solar Energy by Graham Rickard (Wayland, 1990). Comprehensive look at the various ways in which the power of the sun may be harnessed plus instructions for making a solar cooker in the classroom.

The Fragile Earth by John Baines and Barbara James (Simon & Schuster, 1991). Sections on nuclear energy and radioactive waste.

World Resources by John Baines and Barbara James (Simon & Schuster, 1991). Section on the Energy Crisis, Running out of fuel, the Hope of Renewables.

(Both of the above contain sections on a number of areas of environmental concern. They are clearly written and well-illustrated.)

Teachers' Pack

Energy: Economic Awareness and Environmental Education by Ken Webster (WWF, 1990). A secondary school publication with much suitable material for the 11/12 age range. The emphasis is on activity-based learning linked to National Curriculum targets. Many photocopiable extracts from magazines, cartoon strips, advertisements, maps, experiments etc.

THE FOOD DEBATE

Chemically sprayed or Organically produced?

A field of lettuces may receive up to 45 doses of pesticide.

> A huge amount of lettuce could be eaten every day for a lifetime without anyone suffering any ill effects from residues.

Drinking water often contains large amounts of nitrates from pesticide and fertiliser residues.

> There is evidence that the incidence of stomach cancer is actually lower in areas with high levels of nitrates in drinking water.

The above statements are 'media messages'. Identify different parts of the media and discuss the ways that are used to put across messages so that they affect us in certain ways. Suggest that children request publicity brochures and leaflets from a number of organisations listed at the end of this chapter: Compassion in World Farming, The Fertilizer Manufacturers Association, Chickens' Lib, The Vegetarian Society, The National Farmers Union etc. Study these carefully and discuss the ways in which these organisations are promoting their messages. How would the first two statements above affect our perception of what is good to eat? Have children or their families changed their eating habits through concern about a food scare that has been publicised in the newspapers? Consider too, media images of famine. Do children believe that these always portray the truth about such problems?

The world's population is increasing by about 220,000 people every day, and in many areas food production cannot meet the needs of the people. Many new methods have been introduced to increase food production but these can bring other problems into focus. Ask children to research and then list ways in which farmers and the food industry have attempted to step up food production. Such a list could include the rearing of animals in large numbers, increased use of fertilisers and pesticides, developments in food processing, increased mechanisation, irrigation schemes, selective breeding and so on. These could then be researched, either individually or in groups.

Through their research, children will discover that huge quantities of chemicals are now used on farms. These include artificial fertilisers that contain just the right amount of chemicals needed for crops to grow well and pesticides that are designed to protect the crops while they are growing. These include insecticides which kill insect pests, herbicides for weeds, and fungicides for fungal diseases. Alongside these, fruit trees may be sprayed with chemicals to make sure that the fruit is a uniform size and colour, and that it all ripens at the same time. Chemicals are also sprayed onto crops to prevent mould when they are stored in warehouses.

How much do children know about chemicals on farms? Year 6 children at Little Ridge Primary School in St Leonards-on-Sea, were aware of the processes involved and were able to point to some of the problems: "Chemicals kill plants", "They pollute rivers and streams", "Creatures feed on plants that have been sprayed and then they die."

Talk about food chains. Aphids eat the sprayed crop, ladybirds eat aphids, ladybirds are eaten by insect eating birds who in turn become food for hawks and kestrels. Similarly slugs eat lettuces and are eaten in turn by hedgehogs. Hedgehogs eat huge amounts of slugs and the chemicals in their systems eventually kill them. Children could draw up their own food chains to show the different creatures that can be affected.

The British Agrochemicals Association argue that there are many benefits to be gained from the careful and proper use of pesticides. Without pesticides, they claim, the quantity and quality of crops would be far less and food prices would be higher. They argue that many insects and rodents carry diseases and can pose health risks unless they are controlled. They also feel that pesticides can play a useful role in conservation management when they are used to remove dominant weeds which then encourages a greater variety of wildflowers supporting a wide range of wildlife.

Talk about the pros and cons of chemicals in food production. Some children might like to write to a number of organisations for more information. (See the list of addresses at the end of the chapter.) What do children understand by the term 'organic'? The following poem should promote discussion:

Spray Today, Gone Tomorrow

Farmer Rich
is artificial,
sprays his soil
and crops and pests,

can't be doing
with muck spreading,
weeding, weevils and the rest.

Farmer Poor
has gone organic,
lets his land
live naturally,
won't be adding
nitrates, phosphates,
won't be killing chemically.

Farmer Rich
goes on vacation,
Farmer Poor
cannot . . .

might be green but
not with envy –
peace of mind is worth a lot.

Gina Douthwaite

Only 3 out of 30 children in Year 6 at Little Ridge School claimed to have eaten organic food (apples or crisps) but most knew where it might be bought – health food shops, some supermarkets, organic farm shops. "Best if you grow it yourself", someone said.

Suggest that the children devise a questionnaire for pupils in their school to discover what they know about organic food. Questionnaires could be discussed and designed in groups with a final one prepared from the best ideas suggested by each group. Ask children to think carefully about the kind of answers they are looking for. A question such as "Have you ever eaten organic food?" will result in a "yes" or "no" answer which can later be tabulated in some form. If there is a second part to the question, "If so, what?", this will bring in some useful additional information. Children can also ask opinion questions, "Do you think that organic food is better for us to eat? Please give a reason for your answer." It might also be interesting to put the same questions to parents and to grandparents. Do the results differ in any major way? Try surveying shoppers outside a local supermarket. Ask whether they would be prepared to pay higher prices for organic food.

Other children might interview the managers of local supermarkets, having first investigated the produce on sale. What are the reasons for not stocking organic produce, or for only stocking small amounts? Why are the prices higher compared with non-organic produce? Could supermarkets do more to promote healthier buys?

Some children may enjoy preparing shop window advertisements for organic produce. What information would the posters contain? What would be your eye-catching slogan? Children could also design food packets that promote organic produce. What would the labels look like and what information would be included in the text?

Organic and non-organic produce could be 'food-tasted' by blindfolded children to see whether there is any marked difference in taste. Again the results could be recorded.

ADDITIVES - ARE THEY NECESSARY

Collect empty tins, jars and food packets. Ask children to examine the information on an item of their choice and then to write a report about it. The main points to look for are the name and description of the food, what it's made from, how long it can be kept and under what conditions, its weight, volume or number in the pack, its place of origin, preparation or cooking instructions, the name and address of the manufacturer, packer or seller, any nutritional information.

Pay particular attention to the list of ingredients. Is the product additive free or does it contain a number of additives? Check that children understand why additives are added to food (to prevent food spoilage and maintain freshness, to enhance the flavour or appearance of food, to improve or maintain nutritional value, to assist in the processing or preparation of food).

Many people question the need for additives that enhance the appearance of food. Some of them are used to restore the colour of food after a hot and lengthy canning process which is necessary to kill bacteria. Peas that turn khaki and strawberries that look brown are unacceptable to shoppers. Would children be prepared to eat food that looked different to what they were used to?

The European Community gives additives an 'E-number' but many of these are considered harmful by people who prefer natural foods. There are a number of books that list additives and their numbers, and children could be encouraged to check the food items that they are writing about against these lists. The use of artificial additives in this country has increased tenfold over the past 30 years, and no one really knows what harm may be done to our system over a lifetime of eating mixtures of many different chemicals.

What can children find out about the following additives: antioxidants, anti-caking agents, bleaching agents, emulsifiers, flour improvers, raising agents, stabilisers, gelling agents, flavour enhancers, etc? From the packets, jars and tins that have been brought into the school, put together various possible meals and then list the additives that would be consumed. Why are these additives included and how many might possibly be harmful? Many products are now claiming to be additive free, can examples be brought to school?

Various additives are used in meat products and some of these may be harmful to health. Intensive livestock farming results in animals being reared very quickly. Often they receive hormone drugs which make them grow rapidly plus anti-biotics to stem the infections to which they are prone. Many people believe that traces of these drugs may be found in meat and eggs. Do the children know of places where additive free meat may be bought?

Consider the following poem by David Harmer:

Two Men Talking Chickens

'Sentimental claptrap, stick them in a cage,
we're only talking chickens, cheap meat's the rage.
Why all the fuss, the angry hurtful words,
they're not human beings, simply brainless birds.
They don't need to flap their wings, don't need beaks,
anyway they don't last long, perhaps a few weeks.
Rows and rows of boxes stacked in my shed,
stuff them full of corn, stuff them till they're dead.
I'm not a nasty man, I'm kind and forgiving,
we're only talking chickens, I must make a living.'

Scritch scratch, scritch scratch, hear the tiny claws.
Scritch scratch, scritch scratch, they should be out of doors.

'Now don't start pal, don't begin to shout,
I keep my chickens in a field so they can run about,
so free and so happy, hear them cluck and scratch,
the meat is fresh and tender without any match.
In his factory farm they are caged in by wire,
stacks like giant blocks of flats higher and higher.
Out here they feel the rain, experience the weather,
I don't clip their wings or beaks, don't touch a feather.
I fatten them on natural foods, so generous and giving.
Eventually I slaughter them, I must make a living.

Scritch scratch, scritch scratch, hear the tiny feet.
Scritch scratch, scritch scratch, and still we eat the meat.

David Harmer

Some people claim that battery chickens are healthier than free-range birds because they don't pick up so many parasites. Temperature and lighting are carefully controlled and they are kept under shelter. However, more and more people are starting to believe that raising farm animals in unnatural and uncomfortable conditions is totally wrong. Do children think that how we keep animals matters if they all suffer the same fate in the end? Are we prepared to pay more for poultry and eggs from free-range farms?

In *Meet the Greens* by Sue Limb (Orchard Books, 1988), Lizzie Green is shown round Dewey's battery farm:

> ...she could make out rows and rows of cages. They were tiny little boxes, no bigger than a TV set. And in each box several hens were crammed – four or five to a box – so that they couldn't even move. They grumbled and pecked at one another, stood on each other, and fluttered helplessly with scrawny half-bald wings...

Lizzie decides that she can no longer eat Dewy's Eggs and her mother agrees to buy free-range, providing that Lizzie contributes part of her pocket money towards them. The final sentence asks readers what they think and for younger children (8-9 years) the book is a good introduction to the dilemma posed by factory farming methods.

Suggest that children compose one of the letters that Lizzie sends to Mr Dewey in which she tries to persuade him that keeping chickens in cages is wrong. Use information gathered from research into factory farming. If children feel strongly enough about other areas – keeping pigs or cattle in indoor pens, methods or transportation, conditions in slaughterhouses – they can be encouraged to write letters to MPs, and to newspapers or magazines, expressing their views.

Children could debate the pros and cons of factory farming or put across their views through drama. Act out the sort of encounter that David Harmer writes about in his poem 'Two Men Talking Chickens' or dramatise the scene in *Meet the Greens* where Griffo shows Lizzie and Tom round Dewey's factory farm. Script a scene where an animal rights supporter comes face to face with Mr Dewey. Let them argue from their different viewpoints and then introduce a farm inspector.

VEGETARIANISM

"Animals are my friends ... and I don't eat my friends."
George Bernard Shaw

"If abattoirs had glass walls, people would be vegetarian."
Linda McCartney

The magazine of Farmwatch, the youth group of Compassion in World Farming, states that 1 in 12 adults no longer eat red meat, 1 in 30 are vegetarian, and 1 in 10 teenagers are now vegetarian.

Suggest that children run a survey among both children and adults at their school. Figures can then be produced and a comparison made with those quoted by Farmwatch. Ask vegetarians why they choose to stop eating meat.

Greenscene, the magazine for young vegetarians issued by the Vegetarian Society, conducted a survey of young vegetarians in Scotland to discover the reasons why they'd chosen to give up eating meat. The majority of reasons involved a rejection of the cruelty involved in meat production:

"We live in the country, with farms nearby, so I'm used to seeing calves being taken from their mothers soon after they're born. The cows cry all night and keep me awake – I feel really sorry for them."

Lucy Donovan, 9 years

"I once visited a battery farm and it was sickening. It was all strip lights and rows of cages, half the hens had sores or were losing feathers, and the stench was terrible. That's the kind of experience you don't forget in a hurry..."

Cirdan Heughan, 14 years

"I definitely won't go back to eating meat – factory farming stinks and I don't want to eat lots of fats and chloresterol, BSE and chemicals that are in meat..."

Marianne Harvey, 14 years

Contrast these views with the poem below:

Any Part of Piggy

Any part of piggy
Is quite all right with me.
Ham from Westphalia, ham from Palma
Ham as lean as the Dalai Lama
Ham from Virginia, ham from York,
Trotters, sausages, hot roast pork.
Crackling crisp for my teeth to grind on
Bacon with or without the rind on
Though humanitarian
I'm not a vegetarian.
I'm neither crank nor prude nor prig
And though it may sound infra dig
Any part of darling pig
Is perfectly fine with me.

Noel Coward

Suggest that children debate the rights and wrongs of eating meat. For example, large areas of land are used to grow crops as feed for animals destined for human consumption. Yet the same amount of land could feed far more people if it were used to grow crops for <u>direct</u> human consumption. Should vegetarians go further and refuse to wear leather or suede? What about vegans who refuse to eat any animal products whatsoever?

Talk about the problems of being vegetarian when you are a child in a family, dependent on others to provide for your needs. If there are vegetarians in the class, have they any experiences of this? How did their families react to the news? Are there any completely vegetarian households?

Children could act out situations in which a member of the family has decided to give up meat. Think how other family members would react.

Are there vegetarian meals on offer in the school canteen? If not, is this because they would prove a problem or is it simply because no one has ever requested them? Some children might interview the school cook and ask for her opinions on the issue.

Children may care to consult vegetarian recipe books and to draw up menus which show the wide range of dishes available to non meat eaters. Some of these could be prepared, cooked and commented on. A book of favourite recipes could be compiled. Can children find out anything about alternatives to meat e.g. textured vegetable protein (TVP) or fungus foods. A report on 'Man-made meat' is featured in *Food for the World* - Facing the Future Series, by Su Swallow (Cloverleaf/ Evans Brothers, 1990).

WORLD FOOD PROBLEMS

For millions of people in the developing countries of the world there is only one problem regarding food, how to get enough of the right sort of food in order to stay alive. It is difficult to comprehend how each day 35,000 people die from hunger. Many of these are children who die after just a few days or weeks.

Check that children know the right foods that are needed for growth – proteins, carbohydrates, fats, vitamins and minerals. Prepare a display that shows examples of foods from the different groupings. Some foods, of course, will be in more than one category. What happens when all or some of these foods are undersupplied?

Ask children to bring to school newspaper reports concerning hunger in different countries and mark these on a large map. From these reports, can they discover common factors that will give an insight into why there are shortages of food? They will probably come up with some of the reasons outlined below:

1. Many countries will be in Africa where the population is currently growing faster than in any other continent, but alongside population growth is the disappearance of huge areas of fertile land. This is especially evident in countries that border the Sahara Desert where a rise in global temperature, caused by pollution gases, has led to a spreading of desert conditions into some of the world's poorest countries – Mali, Chad, Mauritania and the Central African Republic.

2. In addition to this problem, the best land in many Third World countries is not used to grow food for the local population. Instead, it is used to grow food for export so that these countries can pay off interest payments on the massive debts that they owe. These 'cash crops' – sugar, peanuts, bananas, pineapples, cocoa – are sold overseas at prices which are far lower than the developed countries then charge for their products. (Ask children to make lists of food items that they think come from Third World countries and then to bring to school food labels, packets and tins for a class display.)

3. It is often physically difficult to get food to hungry people because road conditions are bad or there is a shortage of suitable vehicles to transport the supplies. Bureaucracy can hold up goods at the ports or else food is hijacked and sold for profit.

4. Some countries are at war with a neighbour or caught up in a civil war where one group of fighters will refuse to let supplies through in case they fall into the clutches of the opposition.

For these reasons and others, when drought and famine hits an already impoverished country, there are no reserves to fall back on. Relief aid helps temporarily but does nothing to ensure that the problems won't recur.

Talk about the problems that Third World countries face and then on paper or on the blackboard, draw the outline of an imaginary country. The country should be completely land-locked and at war with one or more of its neighbours. Ask children in groups of four to draw similar outlines of imaginary countries and to indicate friendly or unfriendly neighbours. On each map mark in major routeways through the country and a number of main towns. Mark in mountain ranges, rivers, areas in league with the country's enemies and three areas where there is famine on a large scale. Name everything that has been marked on the map and if desired, give it a grid for ease of reference. Finally, point out to each group that the country's major airport is in rebel hands.

Divide each group of children into two pairs with one pair acting as aid workers and the other as rebels. The aid workers' task is to think of ways in which food can be brought into the country and then transported to regions where there is famine. The rebels, meanwhile, will be thinking of ways in which the aid workers' plans can be thwarted and supplies diverted. Which group can think up the most convincing schemes?

Pairs of children can then present their arguments to the rest of the class so that a vote may be taken as to whose plan is more likely to succeed.

Other tasks can also be set regarding the imaginary countries. An inventory of the country's assets – coal, oil, gas, precious metals and so on could be drawn up and consideration given as to the best ways to exploit these. Children might also consider what long term solutions might be found for their country's problems – irrigation schemes, tools and machinery, better education and health care, solving of debt problems so that food crops for people could be grown instead of cash crops.

It is important for children to understand that in reality this is not an 'us' and 'them' situation. It isn't a question of Third World countries getting it all wrong. Victims of famine are often suffering through no fault of their own. They may be members of small farming communities who were living self-sufficiently until their land was taken over by a huge plantation which would produce vast quantities of cash-crops. They may be displaced through fear of invasion or through a drought which withers their crops. At that point the only answer is to get up and move:

There Is No More

The crops are all dead.
The land is burnt dry.
There is no more water.

The farmer is defeated.
His family go hungry.
There is no more food.

Walking for miles.
Nowhere to go.
There is no more home.

> They arrive at the camp.
> Half dead and tired.
> There is no more hope.
>
> A world split in two.
> The rich and the poor.
> There are no more equals.
>
> **Richard McKenzie and Chris Barrett**, 11 and 10 years
>
> (From *The Earthsick Astronaut*, Puffin, 1988)

Discuss how individuals can respond to the problem of lack of food in Third World countries. How effective will these measures be? Talk about how the first step should always be to learn more about situations and what causes them. Suggest that children write for further information. Addresses of organisations connected with food emergencies are listed at the end of this chapter. Point out how aid from the developed nations has changed over the years. Previously it was assumed that less developed countries needed to be industrialised and massive programmes of dam building and road construction were initiated. These often merely served to displace more people from their homes. Today it is realised that the best aid that can be given is through helping small communities to become self-sufficient, ensuring that the yearly cycle of famine can be halted as more and more crops are grown. (Links could be made here with discussions on what constitutes good or bad development in the chapter on 'Development or Vandalism?'.)

Ensure too, that children understand that there is enough food in the world to feed everyone to a reasonable standard and that the problems stem from a) greed and b) difficulties in getting the food to where it is needed at the right time. Children will have probably heard the terms 'butter mountain', 'grain mountain', or 'wine lakes'. What do they understand by these? Have they any idea of the complex reasons why this extra food is not sent to feed starving people? Can a fair system of sharing ever become a reality?

Moira Andrew's poem 'No Connection' helps to put the problem into historical perspective. Is the bleakness expressed in the last verse ever likely to change for the better?

No Connection

Always shy, only the thought
of starving children drove her
to rattle cans in the street.

'Eat it up,' she would say,
eyeing leftovers on my plate.
'Remember the Black Babies.'

For my money the Black Babies
were welcome to cold swede and
bacon rinds. I was full up.

My child's clear logic said
that even if I ate everything
no one would be better off.

Gran would have grieved for
those skin-and-bone photographs
with their huge empty eyes.

And still mountains are
immovable, we're all dieting,
and still the children die.

Moira Andrew

Addresses for Further Information

Chickens' Lib, PO Box 2, Holmfirth, Huddersfield HD7 1QT

Christian Aid, PO Box 100, London SE1 7RT

Compassion in World Farming, 20 Lavant Street, Petersfield, Hants GU32 3EW

Oxfam, 274 Banbury Road, Oxford OX2 7DZ

The Fertiliser Manufacturers Association, Greenhill House, Thorpe Wood, Peterborough PE3 6GF

The Henry Doubleday Research Association, The National Centre for Organic Gardening, Ryton-on-Dunsmore, Coventry CV8 3LG

The National Association of City Farms, Avon Environmental Centre, Junction Road, Brislington, Bristol BS4 3JP

The National Farmers Union, Agriculture House, Knightsbridge, London SW1X 7NJ

The Royal Society for the Prevention of Cruelty to Animals, The Causeway, Horsham, West Sussex RH12 1HG

The Soil Association, 86 Colston Street, Bristol BS1 5BB

The Vegan Society, 33-35 George Street, Oxford OX1 2AY

The Vegetarian Society, Parkdale, Dunham Road, Altrincham, Cheshire WA14 4QG

UNICEF-UK, 55 Lincoln's Inn Fields, London WC2A 3NB

READING RESOURCES

Poetry

The Earthsick Astronaut, selected poems from the Observer National Children's Poetry Competition (Puffin, 1988). Children's views on a large number of issues including factory farming and famine.

The Last Rabbit edited by Jennifer Curry (Methuen/Mammoth, 1990) includes 'Musings of a Battery Hen' by David Money (14), 'The Countryside' by Gordon Dwyer (16) and 'Consider' by Jenny Craig.

What on Earth...? Poems with a Conservation Theme, edited by Judith Nicholls (Faber, 1989). Includes 'Harvest Hymn' by Judith Nicholls and 'Song of the Battery Hen' by Edwin Brock.

You Just Can't Win Poems of Family Life, selected by Brian Moses (Blackie, 1991). Includes 'Cousins' by John Rice (inequality of food distribution).

Fiction

Attila the Hen by Paddy Mounter (Doubleday, 1989/Yearling, 1991). Attila is a big stroppy hen who has no intention of being cooped up in a dirty, smelly battery farm. She plans a daring escape for herself and all her sisters.

Non-fiction

Animal Kind (Early Times/Puffin, 1991). Two chapters 'Animal Farm' and 'Could you be a vegetarian?' will promote much discussion as to the ways in which we treat farm animals.

Children Need Food by Harry Undy (Wayland, 1987). Focuses on the importance of food for healthy growth, then examines how children's lives can be changed completely through being supplied with the wrong kind of foods. Also looks at problems of food distribution.

Farming and the Environment by Mark Lambert (Wayland, 1990). Section on 'Farming and pollution' with good example of effects on food chains. Also, 'Farming for the Future', the organic alternative.

Feeding the World by Clint Twist (Wayland, 1990). Well-illustrated examination of agricultural practices throughout the world. Good section on fishing and fish farming.

Food and Farming by Sue Becklake (Franklin Watts, 1991). Another in a useful series on 'Green Issues' from Watts. Covers problems with agricultural progress plus food and farming in the developing world.

Food for Thought by Gill Standring (A & C Black, 1990). Useful sections on chemicals versus organic, free range versus battery farms, plus soils and rainforests.

Food for the World by Su Swallow (Cloverleaf/Evans Brothers, 1990). Good survey of present trends along with a look to the future: 'Under glass in the desert', 'Camels: our hope for the future', and 'Dining in space'.

Food or Famine by Christopher Gibb (Wayland, 1987). Deals with various myths about hunger and then focuses on the African problem before examining food production and famine in other areas of the world. Also asks questions about the effectiveness of aid programmes.

Poisoned Food? by Tim Lobstein (Franklin Watts, 1990). Excellent survey of the main issues that threaten the quality of our food – fast breeding farms, pesticide sprays, irradiation, fast food, home hazards – plus rules for healthy eating.

The Environment and Health by Brian R Ward (Franklin Watts, 1989). Sections on 'Do you know what you're eating?' and 'Unwanted additions to our diet' plus a look at the water we're drinking.

The Teenage Vegetarian Survival Guide by Anouchka Grose (Red Fox, in association with the Vegetarian Society, 1992). A really practical survey of the theory and practice of vegetarianism. Examines health, economic, human and environmental reasons plus 'The stupid questions people ask', 'The veggie holiday survival guide' and 'How not to wear an animal'.

World Resources by John Baines and Barbara James (Simon & Schuster, 1991). Section on 'The Global Larder' looks at the debt crisis in developing countries and at the success of Chinese agricultural policies.

Magazines

Farm Watch, the magazine of Farmwatch, the youth group of Compassion in World Farming at the address mentioned above. Summer '91 issue includes part one of an A-Z about Animal Rights plus 'Myths about Vegetarianism'. (50p per issue, free to members of Farmwatch.)

Greenscene, a magazine for Young Vegetarians, published by the Vegetarian Society at the address mentioned above. Good cross section of articles. Issue no. 10 features an interview with Paul McCartney, an article on 'Save the Whales' and interviews with young vegetarians in Scotland. (85p, free to junior members of the Society.)

ANIMAL RIGHTS

Although humans are animals too, they generally treat other animals differently to the way in which they treat other humans. Some people believe that the human animal is special and must take priority over other animals, but others believe that all creatures on the earth have equal rights.

Many beliefs stem from religion. The Bible states that man shall have 'dominion' over other animals (although it doesn't say that they may be treated cruelly), whereas Hindus believe that all creatures should be treated 'exactly like one's own son'. Islam forbids cruelty to animals while Bhuddism states that we are all co-inhabitants of the earth.

Suggest that children research the attitudes to animals expressed in religious beliefs. Can they discover anything about the 'spiritual link' that North American natives and aboriginal peoples believe exists between man and animals?

Consider the rights of human beings. Ask children to list what they feel are basic human rights and compare their responses with the Universal Declaration of Human Rights which was adopted by the United Nations Assembly in 1948. This noted that all human beings have rights of freedom and equality. It also prohibited slavery and the slave trade, along with all forms of torture and degrading punishment. Denial of such rights in many parts of the world leads to action being taken by individuals and governments against those countries which are not upholding the United Nations Declaration. Children may be able to think of examples where such action was taken; for example, the sanctions imposed against South Africa, and the boycott of their teams in international sporting events prior to the lifting of apartheid, economic sanctions against Iraq, prior to, during and following the Gulf War of 1991.

Despite action at all levels in response to oppression, human rights are still difficult to enforce. This leads us to question what hope animals can have when they cannot speak out themselves but must depend on human beings to fight for them. Can children extend or adapt their list of human rights and come up with a list of basic rights for animals? The discussions in the sections that follow will show that many animal rights are being denied.

Ask whether children have heard of the word 'vivisection', a general term to describe any experiment on a living animal. Are they aware that over three and a half million animals are used each year in laboratories in Britain?

Children should be asked to consider both sides of the argument concerning experimentation on animals for medical research. Do they know which animals are commonly used in laboratories? In groups they can discuss and then list reasons for and against such activities.

Several reasons are given for the justification of animal research. Scientists believe that knowledge must be pursued and that the suffering and death of human beings has been prevented through research on animals. They point to the fact that many fatal diseases of the past – smallpox, polio, tuberculosis – are now under control through the development of medicines and vaccines which were first tested on animals. Surgeons have learnt about transplant operations and removal of tumours through initial trials on animals.

Critics of animal experiments believe that animals suffer great physical pain and mental stress. They point to the fact that success on animals doesn't automatically lead to success with humans. The bodies of animals are different to ours: humans may safely take the travel sickness drug Meclazine while the same drug causes deformities in rats. Millions of human lives have been saved by penicillin but this drug is poisonous to guinea pigs. Some scientists even believe that medical research has been held back through experiments on animals leading to the wrong conclusions. Many people now believe that far more emphasis should be placed on measures to prevent diseases being contracted in the first place rather than on research to find cures.

The Cancer Research Campaign's latest Annual Report indicates that just 1.6% of research funds are spent on preventative medicine. Can they list ways in which we can attempt to help ourselves by changing our lifestyles. Lists might include giving up smoking, drinking less alcohol, changing to a better diet, less stress, more exercise etc.

Many people may feel that it is acceptable to sacrifice an animal's life so that human beings may be saved, but far fewer people would be prepared to argue that it is right for animals to suffer so that shampoo and soap may be tested. However, people do want to be assured that the toiletries they buy will not damage their skin, hair and eyes.

Some children might like to put across their feelings through writing poetry or prose from an animal's viewpoint, as Charles Thomson does in his poem 'A Laboratory Rabbit'. Alternatively, diary writing could be practised with children producing the kind of diary that might be written by a laboratory animal, highlighting some of the tests that are being carried out. These may well prove to be powerful pieces of writing, particularly if read aloud at a school assembly that explores the issues.

A Laboratory Rabbit

I'm just a laboratory rabbit
    with hair lacquer sprayed in my eye.
I haven't got a tear duct
    so you'll never see me cry.

I've been frequently reassured
    it's within the legal code,
so I really don't mind a bit
    when I feel my eye erode.

I don't need an anaesthetic –
    what's a bit of soap in your eyes.
I don't like to think the price
    of aerosol lacquer might rise.

They can't use human beings
    because the flow of tears
just means the objectivity
    of science disappears.

Now just a word of warning
    for you kids with rabbits indoors.
Experiments like this
    are ruled by very strict laws.

So remember the things researchers
       and animal scientists do
are not the sort of things
       that ought to be done by you.

If things like that were done
       in the home, of course they'd be
denounced as a case of quite
       inhuman cruelty.

You'd be taken to court at once
       by the RSPCA,
and I'd hate to think what the press
       and the neighbours would have to say.

But of course in a laboratory
       the researchers are dressed in white,
so I'd be the first to admit
       that must mean it's morally right.

I'm just a laboratory rabbit,
       I don't expect any praise,
and they only leave the lacquer in
       for a matter of two or three days.

I'm just a laboratory rabbit,
       I look the world straight in the eye,
and I haven't got a tear duct,
       so you'll never see me cry.

Charles Thomson

How do children react to the above poem? The rabbit is portrayed as being remarkably philosophical and tolerant towards those who mistreat it. Why would the price of lacquer be likely to rise if experiments on laboratory rabbits were discontinued? What about the double standards that exist between what goes on behind the closed doors of the laboratory and cruelty to animals in the home? Is it morally right to be cruel to animals in laboratories?

Are children aware of the publicity being given to cruelty-free products? Do they know which companies have given up testing their products on animals? Perhaps items can be brought to school and examined. Children can also collect leaflets from stores which claim that animal testing is no longer carried out on their products:

TESCO POLICY - WHY WE BELIEVE ANIMAL TESTING IS NO LONGER NECESSARY

Throughout the world the selection of product ingredients that have already been tested on animals and proved safe is so extensive, Tesco believe in the current circumstances that it is not necessary to routinely re-test them.

So, by restricting the household and toiletry ingredients we use to the already-tested selection, we are eliminating the need for us to carry out any further animal testing on the ingredients, or on the finished product.

The founder of the Body Shop, Anita Roddick, has always believed that animals should not suffer in the manufacture of her company's products. All of her cosmetics are tested on human volunteers.

Suggest that children write to a number of shops and stores to ask about their policies towards selling products tested on animals. These might include stores selling cosmetics, household goods or garden products. The following letter was written by Glen Corbett of Millfields CP School, Wivenhoe, near Colchester:

> Dear Sir/Madam
>
> I am a pupil at Millfields School. Our topic is on animals and animal cruelty. I have looked in a book called Animal Rights, there were about three pages with pictures of bad things happening to animals. I read the pages. There was a chimp that was forced to inhale cigarette smoke to see what it did to your health. And there were rabbits that had make-up, shampoo and aerosols tested on them.
> Do you sell any products which are tested on animals?
>
> Yours faithfully
>
> Glen Corbett

Cruelty-free products are often more expensive than those tested on animals. Would children be prepared to pay more themselves and how would they try to persuade others to do likewise? What about families on very limited budgets?

Household products which are labelled 'New' or 'Improved' may have been 'improved' through testing on animals. Children may wish to write to companies who produce these products and ask if animals were involved. If the answer is yes, then a subsequent letter could politely point out that they will not be buying the product until other ways of testing it can be found.

In the children's novel *Adam's Ark* by Paul Stewart (Viking, 1990), Adam's autism is confirmed at an early age and he remains locked in his silent world until he is given a cat as a companion. He discovers that he can 'think-talk' with the cat and subsequently with many other animals, all with sad tales to tell of how their species has suffered at the hands of mankind.

As the story develops we discover a possible link between Dimwell's Research Institute on the edge of Adam's town and the disappearance of many pets from the neighbourhood. Adam's friends are keen to prove that Dimwells have taken their pets and then to find a way of releasing them. Adam, however, faces something of a dilemma for his father works at the research institute. When they do manage to gain entry, their worst fears are realised:

> **Some of the animals had been drugged up and were cowering in the corners of their cages. Others had been strapped into fixed positions to stop them scratching away the chemicals being tested on their skin or in their eyes.**
>
> The story will promote much discussion regarding concern for human versus animal life, as Adam's father suffers a fatal accident when the animals are freed. Adam tries to feel something akin to grief when he finds himself on the shore and yells at the wind, "*MY FATHER, MY FATHER, MY FATHER!!* but the words didn't mean 'my father is dead', they meant 'my father was responsible for all that pain."
>
> Year 6 children at South Avenue County Junior School in Sittingbourne discussed how animals are treated and decided to undertake surveys among members of their families to seek out their views on whether animals should be used a) for testing drugs, and b) for testing cosmetics. The results showed 100% agreement that animals should not be used in the testing of new cosmetics but there was considerable disagreement among those interviewed as to whether it was right to use animals for medical research. Similar surveys may promote valuable discussion on the ways in which questions should be asked, and the results that are received.
>
> Children will be aware that some animal rights organisations have turned to violence to put their points across. They believe that the law should be broken if necessary in order to change the ways in which animals are treated. Bring to school press cuttings about such activities and discuss whether firebombing or scare tactics where food is supposedly poisoned can ever advance the cause of animal rights.
>
> Suggest that children write either an editorial giving their own views about such actions or a newspaper report that gives the 'facts':

LABORATORY ANIMALS SET FREE BY ANIMAL RIGHTS ACTIVIST

Hundreds of animals were set free by animal rights activists while the city was out celebrating Halloween. At the New York laboratory masked raiders broke in with axes and crowbars.

These animals were drugged daily for experimentation. The animal rights activists broke the cages open and put the animals in a van and took them to Central Park where they released them into the wild.

The Chief Scientist denies drugging these animals, despite all the evidence produced by the animal rights activists. They say the animals were being experimented on with medicines. They say, "We have succeeded in rescuing the animals."

Eye witness Doris Dimnallby saw them from the house next door and saw them take off their masks.

Reported by **Ben Davis** (10 years),
West Hove Junior School

THE FUR TRADE

A fur coat looks better on its animal owner than draped around a glamorous woman writes Liz Eburne, 12, of Kent

I AM writing about my feelings on the fur trade. Most people have seen the advertisements 'Rich bitch, poor bitch', but does anyone ever think about the seriousness of the issue that the advertisement is trying to put across?

For the fur coat to be hanging in a shop, some poor defenceless creature had to give up its life. Just so some rich, tasteless woman can show off.

If this coat was made of human skin, then nobody would wear it. Can't they see it is just as bad to wear an animal skin?

I hope other people agree with me and would be willing to express their feelings on the subject or to speak up in defence of the animals that have to suffer.

Liz Eburne, 12, *Early Times*, Oct 31 - Nov 6 1991

Read the preceeding article and ask for children's opinions. What do they know about fur trapping and fur farming?

The view of Lynx, a non-violent organisation dedicated to the protection of fur-bearing animals, is that the fur trade is a "...cruel and despicable business. Because no-one needs a fur coat. They are simply status symbols – luxury garments bought at a heavy price in animal pain and suffering."

In the past decade Lynx have run a very successful campaign aimed at changing society's attitude towards fur. Many pictures of animals caught in leg-hold traps have been circulated and striking posters have appeared which show the unpleasant reality behind the glamour of fur. More than 38 million mink and foxes live their lives in fur farms, "the animal equivalent of the concentration camp" (Lorraine Kay, author of *Living Without Cruelty*, Sidgwick & Jackson 1990). In 1987, when Lynx commissioned a poll by Research Surveys of Great Britain, 71% of the adult population thought there should be a total ban on trapping animals for their fur, 70% wanted fur farms banned and 71% thought it wrong to kill any animals for their fur.

Lynx, PO Box 300, Nottingham, NG1 5HN

The Fur Institute of Canada now say that 90% of animals can be trapped in reasonably humane ways and that it is looking into the development of padded leg-hold traps and soft-holding leg snares. The Fur Education Council (FEC) claim that international regulations have now forbidden the import of fur from endangered species into Britain. The Council also claim that the livelihood of communities in Greenland, Canada and Alaska is threatened by the collapse of the fur trade in Britain.

Recently Lynx held a competition that asked entrants to design exotic alternatives to fur that might be worn for a night at the opera. Children may enjoy designing their own ideas and then talking about them, paying particular attention to the materials that they would use.

What else can children find out about the arguments for and against the fur trade? What can they also discover about other creatures that are slaughtered for their hides; these include lizards, snakes, crocodiles, kangaroos and sharks. Suggest that they write to the various addresses that are listed at the end of this chapter, asking for literature. A display of materials might then be prepared for other classes to visit. If possible make it an active display so that children are invited to think about what they are seeing. Perhaps they might take away and fill in a questionnaire that records their thoughts about the issue. These can then be collected and the results analysed.

It might also prove revealing to try to get some idea of the kind of people who are prepared to profit financially from the misery of animals. John Foster's poem may prove a pointer to the children's own poetry or prose:

Fox Farm

The silver fox,
with glossy fur,
penned in its man-made den,
paces the prison
yard of its cage,
again, again, again.

The farmer sneers:
"Why should I care?
I'm not breaking the law."
The restless fox
prowls without point
a wire-mesh tundra floor.

The fashion-hounds
dripping with scent,
admire and stroke his pelt.
The farmer shrugs,
pleads innocence,
stuffs banknotes in his belt.

John Foster

BLOOD SPORTS

List different animals and the ways in which they are treated. The list will probably be quite a long one – fox hunting, deer hunting, hare coursing, badger baiting (illegal in many countries, including the UK), bullfighting, cock fighting (banned in the West but still very popular in the Far East), dog fighting (many illegal fights still take place) and so on. Children can then discover as much as they can about these practices. Groups can research different areas, letters can be written and sent to various organisations seeking their viewpoints, arguments for and against drawn up and the findings reported back to everyone else. They should then be in a better position to sum up their own feelings about hunting.

The wildlife hunted in blood sports is usually labelled a pest by farmers. Hunting is justified as a way of control. Claims are made that hunting helps to conserve the countryside through the maintenance of habitats.

The League Against Cruel Sports campaigns against the killing of animals for amusement:

Foxhunting has the same purpose as the now illicit pastimes of dogfighting, bearbaiting and cockfighting – to provide amusement for human beings. It is not a form of fox control, nor is it meant to be. The 'control' argument was recently invented to counter the protests of those of us to whom the killing of animals for amusement is morally unacceptable.

There are five thousand gamekeepers in Britain whose task is to preserve game birds long enough for their employers to shoot them out of the sky for recreation.

Read the children Charles Causley's poem 'I saw a jolly hunter' (*Figgie Hobbin,* Puffin, 1979). This poem along with two books by Roald Dahl, *The Magic Finger* and *Danny the Champion of the World*, (Puffin, 1974 and 1977) will promote much discussion about the practice of shooting birds.

In Rosalind Kerven's *Who Ever Heard of a Vegetarian Fox?* (Blackie, 1988), Sarah and her older sister, Caroline, move to the countryside from Leeds and are horrified by the gamekeeper's traps in the hills around them. Caroline starts to sabotage the traps, while Sarah meets the gamekeeper's son Ian, finding out that he too cares about animals. Later she talks with the gamekeeper himself who tells her that he isn't trying to wipe out animals, just cull them and keep their numbers down so that the birds he looks after can flourish. He tells her that other creatures will flourish too – songbirds, rabbis, shrews and voles - all the creatures that foxes like to eat.

Later Caroline and Sarah rescue a fox that has been caught in one of the gamekeeper's traps. Ian agrees to help them nurse it but the girls face a dilemma when they realise that the fox will need fresh meat in the form of birds, rabbits and bats:

> **'But we can't possibly! We couldn't go round killing animals. Not ... not even for *him*. It's against everything we believe in. Isn't there something else he could have?'**
>
> **Ian shook his head solemnly.**
>
> **'Nope. It's fresh meat he needs. I mean – who ever heard of a vegetarian fox?'**

Much discussion should follow as to who has the wild animals' best interests at heart, the animal rights activists or gamekeepers?

EXPLOITATION

Time to stop the photographers' monkey business

Escaping to the sun this Christmas? Even if you are not, a fair number of your pupils will be and the people at Monkey World have asked *The TES* to ask you to ask them a favour. It is this: please, please, don't allow a beach photographer to take a picture of you cuddling a little chimpanzee.

Monkey World is a sanctuary for rescued chimps down in Dorset and Jim Cronin, the director, has a gruesome tale to tell concerning the proclivity of tan-seeking Brits for snapshots of themselves with furry creatures.

Baby chimps may be furry but unless heavily sedated they are not friendly. Mauled about by the average tourist their instinct is to bite. So to stop them the photographers pull out their teeth. And they beat them, drug them and worse. One chimp rescued from Spain and brought to Monkey World had 50 cigarette burns on its face.

It is in Spain that the worst excesses take place, although to be fair to the Spanish Government it passed legislation 10 years ago outlawing the use of chimps as photographers' props. But at £5 a snap a fast-working photographer can make £50 an hour and, in summer, put in a 16-hour day. Earning that sort of cash there is plenty left over to pay off the police.

The practice was made illegal after it was revealed how the photographers got the chimpanzees. A mother chimp will not give up her baby so she must be killed. So too must all other members of a group who try to defend the mother and child. Geoff Francis of the charity Animaline estimates that eight adult chimps are killed for every baby taken.

That is the horror story, the fairy tale is that Monkey World has managed to rescue 11 chimps and house them in a 2 acre reserve. Another four are in a "safe house" in Spain and will soon be shipped to Dorset. Accommodation is being prepared for another 30.

This is where you and your pupils come in. By far the most important point is to get it into people's heads that they must not have their pics taken. But those wanting to do more can adopt a chimp.

The adoption scheme was launched a couple of months ago and already 12 schools and 300 youngsters are involved. It costs £50 for a school, or class, to adopt a chimp but any group wanting to help which cannot raise as much will be welcome nevertheless. If your school does take part, it will receive an adoption certificate and lots of information about the progress of the animals. The life expectancy of a chimp is 40 years so it would be a long-term investment.

Jim Cronin reckons there are about 200 chimps in Spain, most of whom, unless rescued, will be killed at age eight when they become too difficult to handle even when drugged. If they are to be saved a lot of foster parents are needed. Give him a ring on 0929 462537 if interested. Animaline can be contacted on 0983 616980 or by letter to PO Box 10, Ryde, Isle of Wight PO33 1JX.

In fairly horrific terms the above article describes the treatment meted out to baby chimpanzees in order to render them sufficiently cute and docile to be used as childbait by Spanish beach photographers.

I read the article to the children in my class and would have been content to leave it at that. They, however, were not. So fierce was their indignation that I felt duty bound to provide some outlet for it. Thus was a fruitful and immensely enjoyable term's work begun.

It started with protest letters to the Spanish Embassy in London and culminated in a classroom fete which raised enough money to adopt a chimpanzee at Monkey World in Dorset. In between the children learnt about primates, debated animal rights and vivisection, and wrote to several local stores to question their policy on animal-tested products. Their persistence was rather admirable and usually rewarded – only the Spanish Ambassador declined to reply. After a grilling by two of my more intrepid pupils one cosmetic saleswoman remarked, "The children put us to shame, don't they?".

I enjoyed the project for a number of reasons. It provided children with a real purpose for writing; it also demonstrated, in its modest way, that education can serve as a vehicle for practical and positive action beyond the confines of the classroom.

Peter Hanratty,
Deputy Headteacher at Millfields CP School, Wivenhoe

A full account of the activities of the Spanish beach photographers may be found in *Wildlife in the News* by John Craven and Mark Carwardine (Hippo/Scholastic 1990).

CIRCUSES

Attendances at circuses which feature animal acts have declined dramatically in the last decade. While some people are amused by the antics of animals that have been 'trained' to act in ways that are alien to their natures, others label this as cruelty. The sawdust ring may well be an animal's only place of exercise while the rest of the time is spent locked away in 'beast wagons'. There are implications too, that training methods are cruel. Some people also feel that animals are deprived of their natural dignity although others feel that animals have no concept of dignity.

There are many circuses that now entertain audiences with displays of human skills – acrobats, trapeze artists, jugglers, clowns – and children must make up their minds as to how they feel about circuses that still include performing animals. It certainly isn't educational to see elephants or big cats performing party tricks and circuses can't claim to play any part in conservation. What about dolphinaria? Many children will also have views on this subject.

Suggest that children write down their own views about circuses drawing on any personal experiences that they might have had themselves. Organise a debate between the supporters of animal circuses and their opponents. Bear in mind that for a debate to take place some children may have to argue from points of view to which they are opposed. How easy is it to do this? If a circus with animal acts is appearing in the area, some children might like to let their views be known by means of letters to the local papers and the Council.

In the picture book, *Save the Animals* by Wendy Lewis (Cloverleaf/Evans Brothers, 1990), children organise a people circus to raise money which will help save some of the endangered species in the world. Various people offer to participate and each tells of the creatures that they would particularly like to help. Readers are then encouraged to think of more ideas to raise money.

Children may enjoy planning a people circus themselves, making use of the various talents of both children and adults within their school. Decide on a programme of events and advertise this around the school by means of posters. Issue invitations, print tickets and programmes. Perhaps at some stage during the performance, those who feel strongly about animal circuses might like to put their views across to everyone else and to point out that it is quite possible to enjoy a human circus.

Kirsty Stotter

ZOOS

The role of zoos is often seen as twofold: a) to educate the public, and b) to offer secure captive environments to endangered species when their natural habitat is threatened.

Today we can learn far more about animals from television programmes than we can from a visit to many zoos, although there are exceptions to the rule, and a number of zoos have excellent education departments. We can, however, still be misinformed about animals and their habitats. We know that polar bears don't exist in a concrete pit with a pool in and that gorillas don't live alone in small cages. The following poem should promote much discussion on this point:

Catching the Gorilla's Eye

How ever far along
The glass frontage you slide,
He will not look at you,
But strokes back the hair
From a puzzled forehead,
Gazes beyond the faces
Peering and grimacing,
And feels in the distance
Such an intensity
Of green heat, such a
Cacophony of parrots,
That he must shade his eyes.

Theresa Heine

Although many zoos promote conservation, captive breeding programmes are less extensive than we might suppose. There have been some successes but figures from 1986 showed that the list of endangered species in the world totalled 2,422, only 66 of which are part of endangered species breeding programmes. Opponents of zoos say that the money would be better spent protecting the habitats of animals in the wild. They feel that zoo environments are often unsuited to the needs of the creatures and although many zoos now aim for more sympathetic confinement, this must always be balanced against the expectations of paying customers who want to get close to animals.

Children may care to think about this dilemma and to suggest possible solutions. Ideas could be planned out on paper and enclosures that are both sympathetic to the needs of animals and visitors can be drawn or modelled.

Children from Weston Road Primary School in Lewes were offered an opportunity to design the kind of habitat that they believed would be suitable winter quarters for a group of meerkats (sociable animals from the mongoose family). The invitation came from Drusillas Zoo Park at Alfriston and their teacher, Dave Holland believed that the project provided the school with an ideal opportunity to respond to the requirements of the National Curriculum in a meaningful manner:

This was not simply to be a simulated classroom activity. Decisions taken during the project would have a direct bearing on the meerkats' quality of life and the establishment of a stable breeding population. Due to the need for such sensitivity it was decided to approach the task gradually, enabling the children to develop a balanced awareness of the animals' needs before attempting any design work.

The children examined the history of zoos and previous attitudes towards housing animals in captivity. They realised that Drusillas took great care to establish their animals in sympathetic environments. They studied meerkats and learnt about the hostile conditions of the Kalahari Desert which is their natural habitat. Decisions were taken as to features to be included – heating, an area for public viewing, termite mounds, a locust feed etc.

Andrew Prior writes about the project:

THE NEW MEERKAT ENCLOSURE

Western Road Primary school in Lewes were approached by Drusillas Zoo and asked if they would like to be involved in the design of a new enclosure for some animals from the Kalahari desert.

The pupils had recently been taught all about the meerkats and their habitat. Every week for six weeks the children went to Drusillas Zoo to survey the area where the proposed enclosure was to be built. They also visited the meerkats in their temporary home and discussed the project with the zoo keepers. The pupils were told that

> the maximum budget was £10,000, to be used for materials and building costs. The school went armed with the tape measures, pencils and notepads and came back with some enthusiastic ideas. After numerous telephone calls to builders and various suppliers they obtained the relevant information required.
>
> The BBC Newsround team followed the project from start to finish and the meerkats and pupils became TV stars. The project was also featured in newspapers and magazines.
>
> The children worked in groups of four with each group drawing up plans from their own designs. Once this was completed they constructed scale models of the enclosure. Two of the models were taken to Drusillas for approval. The best points were chosen from all the designs to produce the final model. A few weeks later building started and after a month it was completed and the school invited to view it.
>
> The meerkats seem very happy in their new designer home and it is a hit with all the visitors, a very satisfactory conclusion for all those involved in the project.
>
> By Andrew Prior, aged 10
> Western Road Primary School, Lewes

In some zoos, animals are just another attraction along with the funfair and theme park:

> What must go through a Polar Bear's mind as a monorail crawls overhead for the umpteenth time, packed with people listening to a facile pre-recorded commentary? What does a rare and beautiful snow leopard think as it sits a short stone's throw away from the 'Runaway Mountain Train', forever hurtling round an endless tract to the screaming delight of its passengers?
>
> **Will Travers,** *World Magazine*, December 1987

Most children will have experiences of visiting zoos at one time or another. Many will have seen bored or lifeless animals and will have noticed the behaviourial tendencies that they exhibit. Ask them to put themselves in the guise of zoo inspectors and to prepare a report on an exhibit. Prior to this, and working in groups, children can discuss and design a standard report form that might be used in any situation. The form will probably comprise name of inspector, address of zoo, date, time, animal to be inspected, size of cage or compound, special features, sex, age and size of animal, condition, notable behaviour patterns, suggestions etc. Remember, however, that reports may not be totally damming, there may be factors that are adequate or even things that impress.

Alternatively children, either singly or in groups, may care to put their feelings across through letter writing. The two letters below outline both sides of the argument:

> The Animal Liberation Society
> 15 Avenue Road
> Greentown
>
> John Brown MP
> House of Commons
> London
>
> Dear John Brown
>
> I am the President of the Animal Liberation Society (ALS) and along with our many members, I object strongly to the zoo in this town. We in the ALS are taking steps to have the zoo closed down. We hope that you will be sympathetic to our cause and understand how important it is to make a firm stand.
>
> Surely you must agree that all animals belong in their natural habitat and should have the right to live in freedom as nature intended. It cannot be right to sentence wild animals to a life behind bars where they lack space to run freely, where they are unable to hunt their food as they would in the wild, and where they are unable to breed as they are living in an unnatural environment. A life of captivity for these beautiful wild creatures must be condemned.
>
> We, in our society, intend to have the zoo closed down. We are counting on your support.
>
> Yours sincerely
>
> Margaret Blount

West Side Zoo
West Bank Road
Greentown

John Brown MP
House of Commons
London

Dear Mr Brown

As our MP I think you should know that the Animal Liberation Society is trying to close down West Side Zoo.

I am the Head Keeper at the zoo and fully understand the good work it does. It would be a disgrace if it were to be closed down by a group of people who refuse to realise this.

Some of our tigers have been rescued from the wild where, because of a drought, they have been too weak to hunt for food. Even if they survived the drought they had hunters after them for their skins. Our zoo has given them a good home. They are now well nourished, fit, and safe from harm, with plenty of other tigers for company.

Our zoo takes care of a variety of rare species of animals and some of these are breeding successfully. Without the kind of care our zoo offers, these animals would become extinct.

All our animals live in spacious enclosures and as some of them have been bred in the zoo, it would be cruel to return them to the wild to fend for themselves. This is what the ALS intends.

The animals in our zoo are well cared for and contented; it would be a terrible mistake to close us down. The staff would be devastated as they work extremely hard for the welfare of the animals.

Our zoo, because it is recognised as being well run, attracts many visitors to the town. I'm sure as our MP you understand our work and will support us.

Yours sincerely

Simon White (Head Keeper)

It may well prove interesting if children consider these letters and then attempt to write John Brown's replies. What factors would influence his viewpoint?

The animal rights debate could well be extended with older children. Why do some people feel that it is acceptable to treat animals so badly? In his book *Badger* (Teens: Mammoth, 1986), the novelist Anthony Masters reveals the horrors of badger-baiting when Andrew goes to stay with his cousins in Somerset and discovers that his Uncle George is pursuing this barbaric 'sport'. Children could consider what it is that impels human beings to derive pleasure from the infliction of pain on animals.

On a larger scale, we all know that great cruelty exists with regard to animals, and we should ask ourselves if this is because they are *different*. What implications does this have with regard to our treatment of people who are different in some way? Many children will have first-hand experience of racial prejudice, or prejudice connected with religious beliefs. They may have witnessed instances where people who suffer with mental or physical disabilities have been treated badly. Perhaps our attitude to animals is an indicator of our attitudes to people?

Discussion of contentious areas such as these may help to instill a sense of respect for, and recognition of the intrinsic value or worth of each individual, animal, habitat or whatever, and their rights to certain things.

ADDRESSES FOR FURTHER INFORMTION
(Please enclose a SAE)

Vivisection

Animal Aid, 7 Castle Street, Tonbridge, Kent TN9 1BH
Organises 'Living Without Cruelty' Campaign. Educational Emphasis. Youth group.

Animals in Medicines Research Council, 12 Whitehall, London SW1A 2DY
Provides information about the role of animals in medical research.

British Union for the Abolition of Vivisection, 16a Crane Grove, London N7 8LB
National 'Choose Cruelty-Free' Campaign.

The Animals' Defenders, 51 Harley Street, London W1N 1DD
Resources pack for young people available. Issues *The Animals' Defender* magazine.

The Fur Trade

Beauty Without Cruelty, 11 Lime Hill Road, Tunbridge Wells, Kent TN1 1LJ

Compassion in World Farming, 20 Lavant Street, Petersfield, Hants GU32 3EW
Campaigns against fur farming.

International Fund for Animal Welfare, Tubwell House, New Road, Crowborough, East Sussex TN6 2HQ
Anti-sealing campaign.

Lynx, PO Box 300, Nottingham NG1 5HN
Magazine, newsletters, fact sheets.

Chimpanzees in Spain

International Primate Protection League, Claremont Hall, Pentonville Road, London N1 9HR

Monkey World, Nanoose Longthorne, East Stoke, Bindon Abbey, Wool, Dorset
Adopt-a-chimp scheme now running.

WWF UK (World Wide Fund For Nature), The Conservation Department, Panda House, Weyside Park, Catteshall Lane, Godalming, Surrey GU7 1XR.

Blood Sports

British Field Sports Council, 59 Kennington Road, London SE1 7PZ

National Federation of Badger Groups, 16 Ashdown Gardens, Sanderstead, South Croydon, Surrey CR2 9DR

RSPCA (Special Investigations and Operations Department), Causeway, Horsham, West Sussex RH12 1HG
Information on dog fighting, badger baiting and fox hunting.

The League Against Cruel Sports, Sparling House, 83-87 Union Street, London SE1 1SG

Circuses

Captive Animals Protection Society, 36 Braemore Court, Kingsway, Hove, East Sussex BN3 4FG

Zoos

Zoocheck, Cherry Tree Cottage, Coldharbour, Dorking, Surrey RH5 4LW

Zoological Society of London, Regent's Park, London NW1 4RY

READING RESOURCES

Poetry

A Fourth Poetry Book (OUP, 1982) includes 'The Fox Hunt' by Stanley Cook; *Another First Poetry Book* (OUP, 1987) includes 'The Circus Elephants' by John Foster. Both volumes compiled by John Foster.

Figgie Hobbin by Charles Causley (Puffin, 1979) includes 'My Mother Saw A Dancing Bear'. Superb poem, useful for the historical perspective.

Headlines from the Jungle edited by Anne Harvey and Virginia McKenna (Viking, 1990 and Puffin, 1991) includes 'The Travelling Bear' by Amy Lowell and 'The Bear on the Delhi Road' by Earle Birney, along with 'On Watching the Bears in the Bearpits at Berne' by Margaret Potter, 'Polar Bear' by James Kirkup, 'A Souvenir' (seal culling) by John Kitching, 'Circus Elephant' by Kathryn Worth and 'Au Jardin des Plantes' (about a zoo gorilla) by John Wain.

It's A Mad Mad Mad World selected by Helen Cook and Morag Styles (CUP, 1991 and Cambridge Poetry Book Box) includes 'Percy Pot Shot' by Richard Edwards.

The Last Rabbit edited by Jennifer Curry (Methuen/Mammoth, 1990) includes 'A Mouse Lived in a Laboratory' by Kathryn Boydell and 'Mole' by Robert Sykes.

Fiction

The Magician's House Quartet by William Corlett (Red Fox, 1992). The second book in the quartet *The Door in the Tree* explores the subject of badger-baiting when William, Mary and Alice return to the Golden Valley, an area of wild country on the Welsh borders, and discover that this cruel and vicious sport is threatening harmony in the valley.

The Moonstruck Mongrel by Pandora Pollen (Lutterworth Press, 1989). The main characters in this story are dogs. Rollo, an inquisitive puppy is determined to travel to the moon and believes that he has only to gain access to a laboratory for his wish to come true. Once inside the Lankton Centre he discovers quite different research taking place there.

Non-Fiction

Animal Kind (*Early Times*/Puffin, 1991). An excellent review of the ways in which humans use animals, plus what we could be doing for animals.

Animal Rights by Miles Barton (Franklin Watts, 1987). An examination of various issues plus good photographic evidence.

Animal Rights and Wrongs by Lesley Newson (A & C Black, 1989). Children are encouraged to examine the evidence for and against various animal related issues and then to form their own conclusions.

Animal Rights: Points of View by Barbara James (Wayland, 1990). Begins by contrasting human rights and animal rights, examines attitudes towards animals and reviews the various issues. Well illustrated.

Killing for Luxury by Michael Bright (Franklin Watts, 1988). Trapping, fur ranching, hunting, beauty and cruelty, luxury food plus a look at the policies of other countries around the world. Well illustrated in colour.

Let's Discuss Animal Rights by P J Allison (Wayland, 1986). A look at most of the issues plus discussion points and case studies where a retired animal welfare worker, a former medical researcher and a circus trainer give their views.

Teachers' Book

Living Without Cruelty by Lorraine Kay (Sidgwick and Jackson, 1990). A compendium of ideas for cruelty-free cuisine and suggestions as to how the choices we make and the things we buy can end animal suffering.

THE WEB OF LIFE
....

**This we know. The earth does not belong to man;
man belongs to the earth. This we know.
All things are connected like the blood which unites one family.**

**Whatever befalls the earth befalls the sons of the earth.
Man did not weave the web of life; he is merely a strand in it.
Whatever he does to the web, he does to himself.**

Chief Seattle

WHALES

Consider the above statement. All living things – including man – belong to the web of life. The extinction of any one species will affect the whole web. Once creatures are gone, we cannot bring them back. Perhaps mankind can survive without them, perhaps not. Children need to understand the interdependence of all living things and what is happening in the oceans may help with this understanding.

We all need to breathe oxygen and 70% of the atmosphere's oxygen each year comes from plankton in the sea. Over the past 50 years the numbers of blue whales, fin whales, humpbacks and sei whales have been reduced from several million to just a few thousand. These whales used to eat vast quantities of a large species of zooplankton each year and that plankton is now increasing in huge quantities.

Heathcote Williams in his book *Whale Nation* (Jonathan Cape, 1988) quotes from an article by George Small, 'Why Man Needs the Whales'. In this, Small asks a number of questions regarding zooplankton overgrowth. He asks about the effect on the oxygen-producing smaller plankton in the world's oceans, the effect on the colour and reflectivity of the oceans, the effect on the average water temperature of the oceans, on its dissolved oxygen content and subsequently on the earth's atmosphere.

No one yet knows the answers to these questions but as Small writes, "By killing off the whales of the world man is playing Russian roulette with the earth's primary support system. Yes, we desperately need whales to preserve the air we breathe."

This high and mighty God-like dignity inherent in the brow is so immensely amplified, that gazing on it ... you feel the Deity and the dread powers more forcibly than in beholding any other living object in living nature.

Herman Melville, *Moby Dick* or *The Whale*

To Be A Whale

The whale is at home
    at home in the sea

Man stands on shore
    staring through haze
aiming his sight
    at what he longs to be

The whale is content
    Man is not
it is he who slaughters
    what he longs to be

To be a whale
    in the green deep water
to be a natural philosopher
    in an ocean of philosophers

> To be a rolling wet boulder
> > down the valleys of water
> to be one eye open
> > always towards heaven.
>
> **Mick Burrs**

Whales are the largest-brained creatures on earth and many people think of them as our ocean-going equals. Whales have existed for 30 million years – much longer than man, and throughout human history they have been worshipped, sculptured, painted, befriended, feared, loved and commercially exploited. The short extract from *Moby Dick* and the poem by Mick Burrs reflect on our ambivalent relationship with whales and may well provide a starting point for a discussion on how children feel about whales.

Throughout the centuries, the trade in whale products brought prosperity to many nations but modern methods have meant that more whales have been killed in the last 70 years than in the previous four centuries. In 1985, representatives of over 40 countries which had previously signed an International Whaling Agreement, decided to call a halt to all commercial whaling. However, the hunting of whales for 'scientific research' is still permitted, and Japan and Norway continue to hunt whales via this legal loophole.

It may well be useful for children to research the history of whales and whaling. Brainstorm first so that everything that is known already can be listed and then suggest that different groups tackle the different areas – types of whales, primitive hunters, ships and weapons, the whaling industry, modern hunting, conservation etc. Once information has been collected children can prepare a display or report back to the other groups. Information collected could also be placed in a data bank.

Children may well discover that the International Whaling Agreement only lays down rules for the large whales; the smaller ones, including dolphins and porpoises are not protected at all. Around Japan's coasts, thousands of dolphins are killed each year and thousands more die from drowning when they become trapped in tuna fishermen's nets. (Many tins of tuna now contain statements that the tuna has been caught with a pole and line. Suggest that children write to these companies and ask how they can be certain of this.)

Every year in the Faroe Islands, pilot whales are slaughtered in a ritual known as the *grind*. Using motor-powered fishing boats the islanders drive a pod of whales into a small bay and then kill them with knives or scythe-like hooks. Up to 500 can be killed at any one time, including young or pregnant whales, as the sea turns red with their blood.

This barbaric ritual has been taking place for over 400 years. However, originally the islanders were heavily dependent on their whale catches. Most of the carcass of the whale would have been used – the flesh eaten or salted and stored, bones made oarlocks and tools, skulls were used for fences and the blubber converted to oil.

Today, however, very little of the whale is still used. Small portions of the tenderest meat are eaten but much of the whale is left to rot. Supermarket shelves in the islands are full of a wide variety of foods and it seems senseless to carry on the slaughter. Indeed, leading international conservation agencies have been trying to persuade the Faroese to stop. Concern is expressed about the cruelty involved and about the future of pilot whales as a species. However, the government still claims that whale meat is necessary and that the culling is a national tradition which the islanders don't want to stop.

Sean Whyte, the crusading director of the Whale and Dolphin Conservation Society, writes that the Faroe islanders consider the annual slaughter to be '...very much a macho sport'.

How do children feel about this view? Are there other activities where such a notion is linked with cruelty to animals?

Michael Morpurgo's novel, *Why the Whales Came* (Heinemann, 1985/Mandarin, 1989) is set in the Isles of Scilly during World War One. Gracie and her friend Daniel befriend the Birdman, someone they have been warned to stay away from. One afternoon they discover the Birdman with a beached narwhal, trying to get it back to the sea. They are desperate to help, but the islanders believe that the whale belongs to everyone:

... we don't much care what this thing is. Whale, narwhal, it doesn't matter to us. All that matters is that there's meat on it and ivory too by the look of it. That's money to us, ... Anything washed up on our beaches is ours by right, always has been ...

Finally the islanders decide to help refloat the whale when they hear how the Birdman and his mother witnessed a previous massacre on Samson Island and how greed and cruelty led to starvation, disease and the death of Samson as a place to live. Then while they make the attempt more whales head towards the beach and a way has to be found to turn them back.

There are many examples of whales beaching themselves and no one is sure as to why they do this. Children could research instances where this has happened around the world and look for similarities in the different situations. Some children could produce a list of ways in which first-aid can be given to such whales. They are in great danger as their immense weight can kill them, they can drown in shallow water and they can swallow too much salt. At a recent incident in Australia, whales were loaded onto trucks and driven to the next bay where there was deeper water. Can anyone design special whale rescue apparatus?

In October 1988 a whale rescue on a far larger scale was undertaken in Alaska when three California Grey Whales were trapped by ice. They were first discovered by Eskimos who accepted that the whales would die and did nothing. Eventually, as the news spread, the Eskimos were persuaded to help keep the whales alive. Suddenly the story became front page news all over the world. A huge bulldozer tried to break the ice and cut a channel to the sea. A sky-crane helicopter tried to smash the ice with a concrete 'bomb', but the whales stayed put. Finally they were freed by a Russian ice-breaker.

Adrian was impressed with the way that nation's co-operated in order to find a solution to the plight of the whales:

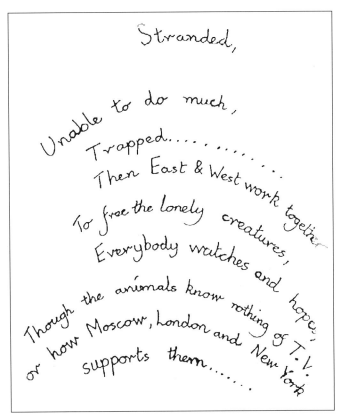

Stranded,
Unable to do much,
Trapped..........
Then East & West work together
To free the lonely creatures,
Everybody watches and hopes,
Though the animals know nothing of T.V.
or how Moscow, London and New York
supports them........

Adrian Harris, 11 years

Suggest that children look and listen out for other instances of international co-operation over environmental matters, where countries have worked together to avoid catastrophe. Some children may care to write about them in the form of a poem. Alternatively a newspaper report could be written giving the facts of the case or an editorial that offers the writer's own views. On the day following the whale rescue outlined above, the editor of *The Daily Telegraph* wrote that ruthless diplomatic and commercial pressure upon the Russians and Japanese to stop murdering whales in their hundreds would achieve much more for the species than helicopters over Alaska.

Children may care to design a board game which, besides being fun to play, also gives information about whales and whaling. Such a 'Whale Trail' will probably involve a journey from A to B; perhaps the annual migration of the Blue Whale swimming south to calve and then north to feed, or the Grey Whales swimming over 19,000 kilometres from the Arctic to Mexico. The game's objective could be to reach the breeding grounds in as short a time as possible. As with all board games there could be lucky squares which serve to speed up the journey and obstacles or hazards that slow it down. Such hazards might include an encounter with whalers, a collision with a ship and a detour to avoid a huge oil slick. Rules and instructions will need to be written and agreed on. The best test will then be to offer it to another group and see if they can play it successfully.

The following piece by Marian Swinger looks back from the year 2150 to a time when whales became extinct:

Natural History, April 25, 2150

Yes, children, just one hundred years today
the last whale on the planet passed away.
You've seen them in your books and on T.V.
those huge dark shapes beneath the blue-green sea.
Massive as they were, they loved to play,
leaping, splashing down; great plumes of spray
would mask the mighty bodies, metres long.
Underneath the ocean, there was song
as whales called to each other, oceanwide.
You'd think in all those fathoms, they could hide
from treacherous humans, but this wasn't so
for where the whales went, whaling boats would go.

> Pursued, harpooned, dismembered, they declined.
>
> We saw how, (on our screen) the last one pined,
>
> a grieving monster in an empty sea,
>
> till death came as a friend and set her free.
>
> We're going to send a message back in time
>
> which says, "Please save the whales - prevent this crime!"
>
> We're sending it to 1995.
>
> It's not too late to help them to survive.
>
> **Marian Swinger**

The above poem might serve as a stimulus to the children's own thoughts concerning strategies for saving the whales. Will we be saying in 200 years time, 'Once upon a time there used to be whales...' or will these creatures still populate the world's oceans? If we imagine the worst, children might like to prepare a radio programme or TV documentary on the fate of the whales as if it were being broadcast in the year 2150. The broadcast might include much of the material that the children discovered when they originally researched whales, plus a look at what happened in the next fifty years. Imagine an interview with the last whale. Would the creature feel resentment towards mankind? Remind the viewers or listeners that 'Extinction is Forever' and suggest lessons that may have been learnt from the catastrophe.

Alternatively, record the message that is being sent back in time to 1995. What will it say? Is there any chance that it will be heeded?

THE IVORY TRADE

One fact that children may have discovered from their research into whales is that a blue whale can weigh as much as thirty elephants. The elephant is the biggest creature on land, weighing about 4 tonnes and standing up to 4 metres tall.

What can children discover about elephants and how much do they already know about the ivory trade? In groups they could research such areas as family life, habitat, birth, young elephants, courtship, the market for ivory, and the elephant itself – ears, trunk, tusks, etc.

A useful source of reference and an excellent read in itself is *The Elephant Family Book* by Oria Douglas-Hamilton (Picture Book Studio, 1990). The author is one of the leading authorities on elephants and through the story of baby elephant Crooked Trail and his family we learn much about elephant social life, how they love their young and form close-knit and caring families. Some superb photographs accompany the text.

In the 19th Century there were over 10 million elephants in Africa but by 1970 the number had fallen to 2 million. In 1989 there were only 600,000 and as many as 100,000 are being killed annually.

Some governments (including Zimbabwe, Botswana, Malawi and Mozambique) still cull small numbers of elephants each year as they claim a need to keep the population under control. This is because more and more land is being cultivated and the elephants' natural habitat is shrinking. In some areas, numbers are very healthy, partly due to the government grogrammes which allow local people to benefit from elephants, for example, through income from wildlife tours or hunting safaris. The locals then take an active interest in protecting the elephant population.

Ivory prices have increased over 900% since 1970 and although a poacher would only receive a small portion of the market price, money from the tusks of one elephant would still be as much as most of his countrymen would earn in one year. However, big businessmen behind the scenes make huge profits and greed fuels the trade in ivory as elephants are systematically and ruthlessly exterminated.

People have got to realise that if they look at ivory they are no longer seeing a beautiful thing, but a slaughtered elephant and an orphaned baby.

Daphne Sheldrick (Quoted in *The Elephant Book*, Walker Books, 1990)

Suggest that children obtain up to date information about the position of elephants in Africa today. This can be obtained by writing to WWF UK (the address may be found at the end of the chapter). They could then try to publicise the plight of elephants through posters or even a school assembly that celebrates the elephant. Advise people never to buy jewellery, chess sets, billiard balls and trinkets that are made from ivory. Poems and prayers can speak of hope for the future while mock interviews with environmentalists and poachers can put across different viewpoints. Even poachers have families and may have been driven to hunt elephants through lack of money.

Children who wish to speak out further could write letters to acquaint prominent people with the facts of the ivory trade. The main market for ivory is the Middle East and Far Eastern countries such as Japan. Suggest that children write to the leaders of some of these countries and speak out for the elephants. These can be sent via the country's embassy at the United Nations, United Nations Plaza, New York, NY 10017. World leaders do need to hear public reaction to their policies.

Other letters could be written to local MPs urging them to support funding for elephant conservation and to ensure that a ban on trade in ivory stays in place. Letters can also be sent to the editors of local papers outlining what individuals can do to ease the plight of the elephants.

The following poem by Irene Rawnsley may serve as a stimulus to children's own writing. Each verse in the poem begins with "This elephant..." and then gives us information about the creature as it appeared in a television documentary. The final two lines are something of a shock. Some children might like to write in a similar way about other endangered animals - 'This rhino...', 'This whale...', 'This panda...'.

This Elephant

lives on a reel of film
in a tin container.

This elephant
eats leaves
and green bananas through
an hour of documentary.

This elephant
likes mud,
enjoys a squirt at waterholes
with her companions.

This elephant
loves her calf,
charges cross-tusked
at cameras come to shoot it.

This elephant
walked for miles

> on ancestral elephant tracks
> to appear on tonight's TV.
>
> This elephant
> died for ivory yesterday.
>
> **Irene Rawnsley**

An item in volume 2 of *Moonlight First Encyclopedia: The Animal World* (Moonlight Publishing, 1991) suggests that in some instances plants may be able to save some animals from extinction. For many years the Amazonian Indians have been producing jewellery from a plant which appears to be a convincing ivory substitute. Scientists have now discovered that oil from the jojoba plant is equally as good as sperm whale oil when used in automatic gearboxes in cars. How could children find out more about these substitutes, and how effective do they think they might be as alternatives?

TURTLES

For millions of years, sea turtles have been migrating in their thousands across the oceans of the world towards soft sandy beaches where they can lay their eggs. In his adult novel *Turtle Diary*, Russell Hoban writes of the green turtles who migrate from feeding grounds along the coast of Brazil, swimming 1,400 miles to Ascension Island in the South Atlantic "...half way to Africa... Ascension Island is only 5 miles long. Nobody knows how they find it."

Ask the children to find Ascension Island in the atlas and to suggest theories as to how the sea turtles manage to navigate so accurately. They could think of one theory that might be a scientific possibility and a second that is wildly improbable!

In many countries, turtles have long been in demand for their shells which are fashioned into ashtrays, their meat for turtle soup, and their eggs. There is now an international Sea Turtle Conservation strategy which aims to stop international trade in turtles and increase their numbers.

Laganas Bay on the island of Zakynthos (Zante) in Greece is now the most important known remaining nesting area for loggerhead turtles in the whole of the Mediterranean. In the last fifteen years, however, there has been a boom in tourism on the island and increased beach activity has meant that many of the turtles' traditional nesting places have been destroyed. John Rice writes about this in the following poem:

The Tourists

The sun sets like a glowing peach
on the holiday beaches.
All night the tourists have fun
dancing under the bright disco lights,
red, green, blue, glowing white, shimmering silver.
They dance to the rhythms of today's top ten.

But just offshore, in the shallow bay,
the Giant Loggerhead Turtle swims unseen,
she is terrorised by the wild music,
she is frightened by the flashing lights,
she is too scared to wade ashore to lay her eggs.

For two nights she has tried to crawl
from sea to sand to dig an egg nest
with her ungainly paddles.
But the tourists and the teenagers
light beach fires for their barbecues
and their motorbikes scream with menacing voices.
The turtle is confused, she is frightened.

Close by her mate is dying.
Some nights ago, whilst feeding
near the shoreline,
he swallowed the tattered handle
of a carrier bag.
The harsh plastic cuts the soft insides of his stomach.
He can not digest it, he can not feed.
Within days he will die – in great pain.

> Just under the surface of the blue bay
>
> the Giant Loggerhead Turtle treads water, and waits.
>
> No more than a quarter of a mile away
>
> she waits and remains unseen.
>
> Blind as rocks and deaf as sand
>
> the tourists continue with their cheap fun.
>
> On and on, into the night, into the morning,
>
> into the fate of the future.
>
> **John Rice**

Ask the children to comment on this poem. How does the poet let us know which side he is on? What are the things that frighten the turtle and discourage her from coming ashore? What is implied in the last two lines of the poem?

In January 1987 a presidential decree was passed which aimed at providing protection for the Zante turtles and their nesting beaches. Ask children in groups to discuss and then write down what they think might have been the eight points in this decree. Remind them that the turtles bury their eggs on the island's beaches. Compare their ideas with the ones below:

1. Do not use the protected beaches of Laganas Bay between sunset and sunrise.
2. Do not stick beach umbrellas into the sand of the turtle nesting zones.
3. Take your rubbish with you when you leave the beach.
4. At night, electric lights disturb and disorientate the nesting females and discourage others from coming ashore.
5. Do not take motor vehicles, including motor cycles, mopeds and bicycles onto the protected beaches.
6. Do not dig up turtle nests – it is illegal.
7. Baby turtles should never be handled or carried to the sea.
8. A law for sea traffic prohibits all boats from part of Laganas Bay.

How effective will this decree be? There is an obvious conflict between tourism and environmental concerns, with many people set to benefit from tourism. Will the laws be flouted? Children may enjoy designing protection areas for turtles. What would they include?

Turtles are declining in numbers wherever they are found. On a four mile stretch of beach in French Guyana only 4 in 100 baby turtles make it to the sea. In some areas, however, artificial hatcheries are being created in order to boost the turtle population. In this way 75 out of 100 turtles will reach the sea.

For information on turtle conservation in Pakistan and first hand reports from Zante, it is worth reading 'The Battle for the Beaches' in *Wildlife in the News* by John Craven and Mark Carwardine (Hippo/Scholastic, 1990).

ENDANGERED SPECIES

Discuss and then list reasons why thousands of plants and animals are labelled 'endangered'. Such lists may well include: hunting, loss of habitat, pollution, introduction of alien species which prey on indigenous population e.g. dodos on Mauritius, crop spraying and so on.

On a lighter note, children may like to consider the needs of animals that are displaced from their homes for one reason or another. Can they design the sort of advertisements for new homes that different creatures might place in 'The Animal Times'. Such adverts should outline the plight of these creatures and list their requirements. Eye-catching slogans will help to catch the attention of those with homes to offer. Replies might also be written by creatures that are genuine in their desire to help – a mouse might be ill-advised to take up a snake's offer of accommodation!

Fortunately there are success stories in the fight against extinction. 'Operation Tiger' has brought these big cats back from the brink through the creation of special reserves where the tigers can breed in safety. In Britain over 50 ospreys now breed in the Scottish Highlands each year. (Ospreys became extinct in 1908 but in 1954 a pair from Scandinavia nested again and the RSPB worked hard to build up numbers.) There were fears too that otters would disappear altogether but their numbers have increased over the past 30 years. Can children find examples of further success stories? An excellent source of reference here is *Noah's Choice – True Stories of Extinction and Survival* by David Day (Viking, 1990/Puffin, 1991). Tragic stories of extinction are set alongside encouraging accounts of creatures saved from such a fate. Children may like to write to certain organisations if they need information about specific creatures. In the letter below, Louise and Sarah are seeking information from the Rainforest Foundation:

Fetcham County Middle School
Bell Lane
Fetcham
KT22 9ND
16/1/92

Dear Sir/Madam,

6/7 C of Fetcham Middle School are learning about the Rain Forest as it is our topic. Our class is going to do a talk on animals. I'm doing it on the topsy turvy Sloth. I believe it comes from South or Central America. Sarah is interested in the millipede as she believes it lives in dark damp places. We would appreciate it if you had any information about it that we could use. Hope this will be possible and thankyou it it is.

Yours Sincerely
Louise Brown and Sarah Hoyland

Suggest that children write and illustrate picture books for a younger audience. These can tell how various creatures find their habitats threatened or destroyed by human activity. In Danielle Hardy's book *The Gorillas Save Their Homes*, a group of gorillas sort out a plan that will prevent their trees being cut down.

Children may enjoy devising a quiz to make others aware of the problems facing various species. This could be a multiple choice activity where questions are similar to the one below:

> Q. Where do turtles lay their eggs?
>
> A. a) At sea
> b) In the sand
> c) In patches of seaweed.

Quizzes could be devised to suit various age and ability levels within a school.

Children might also enjoy composing an optimistic reply to the poem below which mimics the song 'Ten Green Bottles': *Ten lazy tigers with nothing to fear/in the tiger reserve where no hunters appear/Nine proud elephants...etc.*

Animals Matter

Ten black rhinos were happy in the sun
Along came poachers and then there were none.

Nine playful dolphins cruising free
Thirty-mile-long fishing nets left none to see.

Eight clever cormorants fishing in the waves
One stinking oil-slick puts them in their graves.

Seven lofty rain forests the home of countless creatures
Hacked and burned because of greed are now just bygone features.

Six gentle spouting sperm whales saw no need to flee
But breathed their last with the harpoon blast in the blood-red boiling sea.

Five clumsy natterjacks tried to cross the road
One big juggernaut left no trace of toad.

Four lively otters in the river were well fed
Herbicides and pesticides soon had them dead.

Three wise old barn-owls used to swoop at night
Destruction of their habitat put them out of sight.

Two tusks of ivory on an elephant belong
Not in the hands of carvers in downtown Hong Kong.

One polluted lifeless world spinning round in space
Is this to be the legacy for the human race?

Eva Askham-Spencer, 11 years

ADDRESSES FOR FURTHER INFORMATION

Fauna and Flora Preservation Society, 77-83 North Street, Brighton, Sussex BN1 1ZA

Friends of Conservation (Elephants), Sloane Square House, Holbein Place, London SW1W 8NS

Friends of the Earth, 26-28 Underwood Street, London N1 7JQ

071 - 490 -1565

Greenpeace, 30-31 Islington Green, London N1 8BR

International Fund for Animal Welfare, Tubwell House, New Road, Crowborough, East Sussex TN6 2QH

The Rainforest Foundation, 2 Ingate Place, Battersea, London SW8 3NS

071- 498- 7603

Whale and Dolphin Conservation Society, 20 West Lea Road, Bath, Avon BA1 3RL

World Society for the Protection of Animals, 196 Jermyn Street, London SW1Y 6EE

WWF UK (World Wide Fund For Nature), Panda House, Weyside Park, Catteshall Lane, Godalming, Surrey GU7 1XR

READING RESOURCES

Poetry

Animals Matter (Puffin, 1991). Selected from prose and poetry by children aged 4-15 years which was sent in to a 'Blue Peter' competition. Sections on 'Save Our Sea-life', 'Elephants, Rhinos and Big Cats', 'Monkeys and Pandas' etc.

Headlines from the Jungle edited by Anne Harvey and Virginia McKenna (Viking, 1990/Puffin, 1991) includes 'The Song of the Whale' by Kit Wright, 'Death of a Whale' by John Blight, 'Dolphins' by Jonathan Griffin, and 'Darkness Comes Again' (Elephants) by Virginia McKenna. (Kit Wright's poem may also be found in his own collection *Hot Dog and Other Poems*, Puffin, 1982, and in *The Last Rabbit* – see below).

It's a Mad, Mad, Mad World selected by Helen Cook and Morag Styles (CUP, 1991, Cambridge Poetry Box) includes 'Extinction Day' by Terry Jones.

The Last Rabbit edited by Jennifer Curry (Methuen/Mammoth, 1990) includes 'Extinction of the 21st Century Dodo' by John Walsh, 'We are going to see the Rabbit' by Alan Brownjohn, 'The Rhino' by Kirsty Butcher (13 years) and 'The African Elephant Speaks' by Emma Neilson (11 years).

Whale Nation, Sacred Elephant, Falling for a Dolphin by Heathcote Williams (Jonathan Cape, 1988, 1989, 1990). Three volumes of powerful poetry and quite stunning photography plus, in the former two instances, a catalogue of quotes and opinions from earliest times to the present day. Ted Hughes wrote of *Whale Nation* as "... brilliant, cunning, dramatic and wonderfully moving, a steady accumulation of grandeur and dreadfulness... a measured unfolding of real things from the heart of the subject."

Fiction

Akimbo and the Elephants by Alexander McCall Smith (Mammoth, 1990). Akimbo is the son of a ranger who witnesses the results of ivory poaching at first hand. He sets out to track down the culprits by becoming an elephant hunter himself. A straightforward story for younger readers.

Changes in Latitudes by Will Hobbs (Pan Horizons, 1989). Told by teenage Travis who is out to find fun during the family holiday in Mexico, while his younger brother Teddy is fighting to save the sea turtles that lay their eggs on Playa Tortugas. A sensitive story that some 12 year olds may enjoy.

My Friend Whale by Simon James (Walker Books, 1990). A small boy makes friends with a whale, swimming with him each night until one day the whale disappears. Sensitive introduction to the plight of whales. (A book that might act as a stimulus for children to write their own picture books for younger children based on what is happening to an endangered animal.)

Sad Song of the Whale by Anthony Masters (Hippo/Scholastic, 1990). Book 2 in the Green Watch series. Green Watch, a father, his two children and their cousin, campaign against the senseless slaughter of animals and the thoughtless pollution of the environment. This story is set in the South Atlantic and like the others in the series, is a good adventure yarn with a green message. (Also *Dolphin's Revenge, Gorilla Mountain* and *Spirit of the Condor*, suitable for children at the older end of the age range.)

The Lighthouse Keeper's Rescue by Ronda and David Armitage (Andre Deutsch, 1989). Mr Grinling is about to be sacked from his duties but his involvement in the rescue of a beached whale earns him a reprieve.

The Lonely Whale by David Bennett and Karin Littlewood (Kingfisher Books, 1991). A huge whale rescues a shipwrecked crew and makes friends with a young sailor called Sam. When the whale beaches itself Sam enlists the crew's help to refloat it.

The Sea is Singing by Rosalind Kerven (Blackie, 1985/Puffin, 1987). Tess hears strange singing from the sea. She discovers that her father is linked to large scale pollution and finds herself torn between loyalty to her father and the message brought by the singing.

The Whales' Song by Dyan Sheldon and Gary Blythe (Hutchinson, 1990). Lilly longs to hear the singing of the whales as her grandmother once did. Wonderful paintings, a picture book for all ages.

Toby's Iceberg by W J Corbett (Methuen, 1990). Toby, a young white whale, has a mission in life: to push an iceberg south to the Equator so that his thirsty friends will have something to cool them down. An enchanting fantasy.

Turtle Diary by Russell Hoban (Picador/Pan, 1977). A wonderful read, told in alternate chapters by William G. and Nearera H. who share the same ambition, to release three sea turtles from 'their little bedsitter of ocean' in the aquarium at London Zoo. Adult read.

Non-fiction

Animals in Danger by David Taylor (Boxtree, 1990). Here the reader becomes involved in obtaining the latest information on 10 endangered animals prior to launching possible rescue missions.

Bringing Back the Animals by Teresa Kennedy with illustrations by Sue Williams (Amethyst Books, 1991). Stories of hope for threatened creatures such as the African elephant, the tiger and the bald eagle. An attempt to show that people who care enough can make a difference.

Close to Extinction by John Burton ('Survival' series, Franklin Watts, 1988). A round-the-globe look at species on the brink of extinction plus a few that have been brought back from the brink.

The Animal World – Moonlight First Encyclopedia, volume 2 (Moonlight Publishing, 1991). An excellent review of animals, their habits and characteristics, from prehistory to the present including a section on animals at risk. Information is clearly set out and well illustrated throughout.

The Elephant Book by Ian Redmond (Walker Books, 1990). Written for the Elefriends campaign with a preface by Daphne Sheldrick. Marvellous photography and quotes along with a fascinating look at elephant families.

The Magic of Dolphins by Horace Dobbs (Lutterworth Press, 1990). Encounters with dolphins in the wild and demonstrations of the affinity that exists between man and dolphin.

The Story of Three Whales by Giles Whittell, illustrated by Patrick Benson (Telegraph Books/Walker Books, 1988). True account of the three Californian grey whales trapped under the frozen Arctic.

Whales, Dolphins and Seals by Patrick Geistdoerfer, and *The Long Life and Gentle Ways of the Elephant* by Pierre Pfeffer. (Both in the Pocket Worlds series from Moonlight Publishing, 1990 and 1987.) These books are packed with fascinating facts about their subject matter plus excellent illustrations. Good for research at the lower end of the age range.

Wildlife in Danger by Malcolm Penny ('Save Our World' series, Simon & Schuster, 1990). Good coverage of whales and whaling, seals and sealskin and trading in animals, plus pollution and loss of habitat. Well illustrated, recommended for 10-12 year olds.

APPENDIX

A Class Museum or Display

The collection has been built up over many years and is made up of finds contributed to the school by people who have a general interest in natural history. The children have found a surprising variety of things and have always shown a capacity for looking in awkward places! Perhaps they see more because they are closer to the ground!

Some memorable items are the ram's skull which arrived complete with wool, skin, eyes etc after spending a week in a black plastic bag in the boot of a car. The result was not very pleasant. A small house mouse was found completely mummified in a rolled up carpet in a loft. The partial fox skeleton is from an animal involved in a road accident outside school. The tarantula died on the set of 'Indiana Jones' where one of our parents was working as a cameraman. He said straight away that he knew of an excellent resting place for the body!

The children use the collection to practise identification and classification skills, and it also stimulates discussion and writing. Many of the more fragile items are now housed in small display cases designed and made by the children.

Philip Hayes, Atwood Primary School, Sanderstead

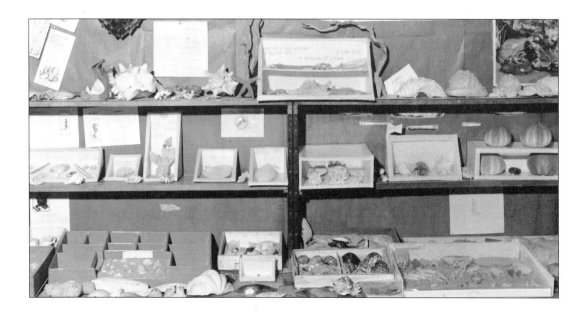

FURTHER READING RESOURCES FOR CHILDREN AND TEACHERS

BBC Fact Finder: Earthwatch by Penny Horton, Tony Potter and Dee Turner (BBC Books, 1990). Well produced and well illustrated examination of environmental problems, from the ozone layer to rainforests, plus practical suggestions.

Dinosaurs and all that Rubbish by Michael Foreman (Hamish Hamilton, 1972/Puffin, 1974). Man leaves our polluted world to travel to the stars. Meanwhile dinosaurs re-colonise the Earth and tidy it up. Man is only allowed back when he agrees that the Earth should be shared and enjoyed by everyone. Again, this will probably promote a lot of questions.

One World by Michael Foreman (Anderson Press, 1990). A lovely book to share with children. The world of a rock pool is a microcosm of the world itself. Prepare for much discussion afterwards. (Also *Books for Keeps no. 62*, May 1990 in which Michael Foreman writes about the slow emergence of *One World* in his article 'The Birth of a Book'.)

The Children's Giant World Atlas compiled by Keith Lye (Hamlyn). A really useful resource when children want to know where the rainforests are or where the latest oil spill has occurred etc.

The Ozone Friendly Joke Book compiled by Kim Harris, Chris Langham, Robert Lee and Richard Turner (Beaver, 1990). A wonderful antidote for anyone who finds themselves taking everything just that little bit too seriously, for example: *What do you harvest from polluted fields? Acid grain.* Be warned!

Specifically for Teachers

Catching the Light – Language and the Environment. A resource book for teachers of Key Stage 1 by Brian Moses (WWF, 1991). Companion volume to *Somewhere To Be,* covering the child, neighbourhood, school, towns and cities, countryside, parks and playgrounds, the seashore, water, waste and recycling, endangered animals.

Earthrights: Education as if the Planet Really Mattered by Sue Greig, Graham Pike and David Selby (WWF/Kogan Page, 1987). Towards 'thinking globally' and 'acting locally'. Useful section 'Beginning Early' focuses on the need to lay the foundations for a 'planet-conscious education programme'.

Greenprints for Changing Schools by Sue Greig, Graham Pike, David Selby (WWF/Kogan Page, 1989). A review of how teachers and others involved in education have set about promoting global education in schools. 'Great oak trees can start in the nursery.'

My World Pack (WWF UK, 1992). A pack containing nine, 16 page illustrated supplements exploring the local environment and making links with global issues. These are aimed at teachers of pupils aged 7-12 years and linked with National Curriculum programmes of study for Key Stage 2 in Science. Teachers' notes are also available. Supplements include: Exploring the Earth, Exploring the Air, Exploring Water, Exploring the Weather, Exploring Plants and Animals, Exploring Ourselves, Exploring Food, Exploring Energy, Exploring the Future. (Originally available as inserts in Scholastic's *Junior Education*.)

The Books for Keeps Green Guide To Children's Books published Spring 1991, price £6.50 from *Books for Keeps*, 1 Effingham Road, Lee, London SE12 8NZ. A review of over 350 works of fiction and non-fiction with a 'green' theme plus articles on promoting environmental awareness in the classroom.

The Green Umbrella written and compiled by Jill Brand (WWF/A & C Black, 1991). Stories, songs, poems and starting points for environmental assemblies. Sections on water, air, living things, people and places, food, energy and waste, and Planet Earth.

The Primary School in a Changing World: A Handbook for Teachers edited by Jenny Burton (Centre for World Developmental Education, 1989). Practical problems and advice regarding the development and implementation of a whole school policy on global education. Useful activity plans.

FURTHER ADDRESSES FOR RESOURCE MATERIAL

Aluminiun Can Recycling Association, Suite 308, I-Mex House, 52 Blucher Street, Birmingham B1 1QU
Free information packs with teachers' files and leaflets.

Christian Aid, PO Box 100, London SE1 7RT
Produces *Focus on Water* – ideas for activities etc.

English Nature, Northminster House, Peterborough PE1 1UA
Produces posters, wallcharts and booklets on all aspects of conservation.

Forestry Commission, Public Information Division, 231 Corstorphine Road, Edinburgh EH12 7AT
Environmental Threats to Forests available free.

Friends of the Earth, 26 - 28 Underwood Street, London N1 7JQ

A range of fact sheets for primary children including free leaflets on acid rain, agriculture, air pollution, energy, global warming, ozone depletion, recycling and water pollution. Also *The Friends of the Earth Yearbook* packed with facts, fun and games, positive things to do and experiments. Friends of the Earth are intending to start a teachers' and schools' membership scheme which will provide subscribers with educational material.

Greenpeace, 30 - 31 Islington Green, London N1 8XE

The Public Information Unit answers letters from all age groups, including young children (probably about 5% of all letters received are from under 10s). A fact sheet about whales is available, along with a poster published by the Greenpeace Environmental Trust called *Where do we go from here?* This introduces children to environmental terms and encourages them to identify the good things and the bad things that are going on in the world.

Save the Children, Mary Datchelor House, 17 Grove Lane, Camberwell, London SE5 8RD

A pack entitled *Refugees* has been specifically created and tested with 7-8 year olds. It is designed to help children understand the concept of refugees and to encourage a positive attitude towards different communities and cultures. *Doorways* is a pack for 9-13 year olds which may be useful for introducing issues of homes and homelessness. Also check out other material including *Resurrecting Rubbish, Trees of Life* and *Hope for the Earth* (about pollution).

The Conservation Trust, George Palmer Site, Northumberland Avenue, Reading, Berkshire RG2 7PW

Produces a set of 20 Junior Topic cards on various aspects of conservation.

The Tidy Britain Group, The Pier, Wigan WN3 4EX

A selection of free leaflets: *Litter, A Problem We Can Solve*. Also *Our Environment*, a project for primary schools, plus a 40 frame filmstrip *Litter, Waste Management and Recycling.*

UNICEF UK, 55 Lincoln's Inn Fields, London WC2A 3NB

Educational materials include *Clean Water: A Right for All*, active project work for 8-13 year olds, cross-curricular A4 project book; *We Are What We Eat, but who controls our choice?*, active learning project on food and nutrition for 8-13 year olds, including photocopiable pupils' sheets and notes for teachers. Also available and co-produced with Save the Children are three project books for teaching about the Convention on the Rights of the Child for use with 8-13 year olds, *The Whole Child, It's Our Right*, and *Keep Us Safe* plus teachers' handbook.

Water Aid, 1 Queen Anne's Gate, London SW1H 9BT
Educational resource materials on water in the developing world.

WWF UK (WORLD WIDE FUND FOR NATURE), Education Department, Panda House, Weyside Park, Catteshall Lane, Godalming, Surrey GU7 1XR
Catalogue includes a large number of publications suitable for the 5-11 age range. Teacher membership scheme.

ACKNOWLEDGEMENTS

I would like to thank the following children and their schools for allowing me to reproduce examples of written work and illustrative material: Gemma Finney, Shaminara Malik, Alexi Gee, Yaron Simpson and Ben Davis, West Hove Junior School; Laura Shuff, Selsdon Primary School, Croydon; Christopher Kinlan, St Saviour's CP School, Westgate; Imogen Hibbert, Adrian Harris and Aaron Turpin, Gallery Young Writers, Rye; Ben Jacques and Nick Kemp, Atwood Primary School, Sanderstead; Shirah Reel, Sarah Cummings, Danielle Hardy, Emma Trigwell, Martina Hardiman and Claire Hoggins, Hammond Middle School, Lightwater; John Wells, Danehill CE School; Emma Warren and Sammy Thomas, Little Ridge CP School, St Leonards-on-Sea; Lisa Butler, Chilton CP School, Ramsgate; Matthew Powell, Forelands Middle School, Bembridge, Isle of Wight; Glen Corbett, Millfields CP School, Wivenhoe; Kirsty Stotter, Freda Gardham CP School, Rye; Andrew Prior, Western Road Primary School, Lewes; Louise Brown and Sarah Hoyland, Fetcham Middle School; Hannah Jane Peckham, Burgess Hill School for Girls.

My thanks also to the following teachers who invited me into their classrooms and/or offered help and advice: Brian Brazier, Little Ridge CP School, St Leonards-on-Sea; Philip Hayes, Atwood Primary School, Sanderstead; Peter Hanratty, Millfields CP School, Wivenhoe; Peter Newbold, West Hove Junior School; Dawn Eldridge, Freda Gardham CP School, Rye; Derek Swaine (Headteacher), Western Road Primary School, Lewes and children from South Avenue Junior School, Sittingbourne and Chilton CP School, Ramsgate who allowed me to print the results of their surveys. Thanks also to Dave Holland, Michael Ann and Drusillas Zoo Park.

The following pieces of writing by children are printed by permission: 'A Threatened World' by Ben O'Malley, 'Dear Mrs Thatcher' by Michelle Millar (from *In Our Own Words*); 'Felling Trees' by Adrian Youd (from *What on Earth...?* edited by Judith Nicholls, Faber, 1989); 'Drowned Valley' by Daniel Benjamin Morden (from *Children as Writers 3*, Heinemann, 1976); Letter - 'Air Pollution' by Megan Fisher (*Early Times*); 'There Is No More' by Richard McKenzie and Chris Barrett (from *The Earthsick Astronaut* - Selected Poems from The Observer Children's Poetry Competition, Puffin, 1988); 'Animals Matter' by Eva Askham-Spencer (from *Animals Matter,* Blue Peter, Puffin, 1991).

Thanks are also due to *Early Times* for permission to reprint 'Sting Saves Rainforests' and 'High Price'; *Survival International* for 'Example of a letter about Yanamami to the President of Brazil'; *The Times Educational Supplement* for 'Time to Stop the Photographers' Monkey Business'; Penguin Books for 'Any Part of Piggy' by Noel Coward, featured in *A Picnic of Poetry* selected by Anne Harvey (Puffin, 1990); W H Allen & Co for limericks by Kate Ashton and Charles Romito from *Great Green Limericks* - Selected Limericks from the Observer Great Green Limericks Competition, in association with Friends of the Earth (W H Allen & Co, 1989); The Department of the Environment for 'The Local Plan Process' (from their booklet - *Local Plans: Public Local Enquiries, A Guide to Procedure*); JJ Douglas Ltd, Vancouver, Canada, for 'To Be A Whale' by Mick Burrs (from *Whale Sound* - An anthology of Poems about Whales and Dolphins, edited by Greg Gatenby, JJ Douglas, 1977).

Thanks and acknowledgement are due to the following writers for permission to publish original material: Moira Andrew, Margaret Blount, Ann Bonner, Pie Corbett, Gina Douthwaite, John Foster, David Harmer, Theresa Heine, Kevin McCann, Robin Mellor, Irene Rawnsley, John Rice, Ian Souter, Marian Swinger, Charles Thomson, Jennifer Tweedie, Jane Whittle, Bernard Young.

All these pieces are reprinted by permission. Copyright of all prose and poetry remains with the authors.

A final thank you to Alison Manners (Education Officer) and Cherry Duggan (Publishing Officer) at WWF for their valuable advice.

If anyone feels that a credit has been overlooked I would be grateful if they would contact WWF so that the omission may be rectified in subsequent editions.

Brian Moses

POSTSCRIPT

From 'Inversnaid'

What would the world be, once bereft
Of wet and of wildness? Let them be left,
O let them be left, wildness and wet;
Long live the weeds and the wilderness yet.

Gerald Manley Hopkins

Go Green,
Keep the Earth clean,
It's my scene,
Know what I mean?

Hannah Jane Peckham, 10 years